WEAVING
WITH
REEDS
AND
FIBERS

A Cluster of Useful Baskets Made from Inexpensive Reeds and Fibers

Among the items shown are hanging flower baskets, a cake basket shaped like a shell, a bread basket with trellis sides and a garden basket.

WEAVING
WITH
REEDS
AND
FIBERS

OSMA GALLINGER TOD
Creative Crafts *East Berlin, Pennsylvania*
and OSCAR H. BENSON

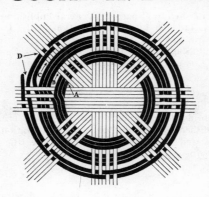

DOVER PUBLICATIONS, INC., NEW YORK

Published in Canada by General Publishing Company, Ltd., 30 Lesmill Road, Don Mills, Toronto, Ontario.

Published in the United Kingdom by Constable and Company, Ltd., 10 Orange Street, London WC 2.

This Dover edition, first published in 1975, is an unabridged republication of the work originally published by Pitman Publishing Corporation, New York and London, in 1948 under the title *Hand Weaving with Reeds and Fibers*.

International Standard Book Number: 0-486-23143-7
Library of Congress Catalog Card Number: 74-16965

Manufactured in the United States of America
Dover Publications, Inc.
180 Varick Street
New York, N.Y. 10014

PREFACE

THIS BOOK is written to meet the demand for a practical handbook in creative hand weaving. Though written primarily for the use of the hand craftsman, it endeavors to supply helpful suggestions for classroom and group instruction. A carefully planned account of the various processes is given in detail, and the projects are outlined for the making of useful, decorative, and salable products.

Weaving supplies industrial training suited to the needs of both young and old. For the former, it connects classroom work with the enterprises of the home, and trains the student in painstaking workmanship; for the latter, it requires no physical exertion save the use of the hands. To both it gives training in co-ordination and manual dexterity. The craftsman gains experience in the handling of shape, color, size, and proportion. He learns to employ discarded materials, weaving old sheets into rugs, fashioning doormats of raveled-out burlap bags, making toys and gifts from rope and wood and wire. He learns to value raw materials found in nature—plant-fibers that may be twisted into rope, cornhusks that can be braided to make mats and baskets, rush that is woven into strong seats for chairs.

A further recommendation for weaving is that it requires no appliances that cannot be made at home. It demands little equipment and small outlay for materials, since reed, raffia, pine needles, grasses, twigs, rushes, cornhusks, and coarse fibers and yarns are practically all that are needed. Thus weaving furnishes an opportunity for making a full- or part-time income, either from the sale of the articles made or by teaching the craft to others. Some vocations depend largely upon the use of the mind, some more upon the

v

use of the hand, and some upon the wholesome co-ordination of both. In this last class the art of weaving ranks high. For this reason it is particularly well suited to occupational therapy. It will unquestionably increase in popularity as a practical activity involving minimum expense and encouraging a maximum of wholesome reactions.

The book is planned to cover six months of home or group study, or nine months of class work. Home and class work may be advantageously combined if desired. Every effort has been made, by close correlation of the figures and the text, to suggest possibilities of further projects beyond those which have been actually described. In instruction of this kind it is important, not only to train the craftsman to do skilled work, but also to stimulate his interest and encourage him in creating new designs and in devising useful articles. In pursuance of this idea, the authors have given many detailed suggestions for the making of small articles such as vases, trays, flower baskets, and mats, on which there is a quick commercial turnover. There are also time-taking projects including the caning of chairs and the making of various types of furnishings. Any or all of these may well suggest even wider possible activities in the fascinating art of creative hand weaving.

OSMA GALLINGER TOD

Provincetown, Massachusetts

CONTENTS

Contents

ILLUSTRATIONS

PART I

Creative Weaving

CHAPTER 1

HISTORY OF THE WEAVING ARTS

NO MATTER how far back we go in history, we find basket-making among industrious peoples. In biblical times sacrifices were offered in baskets. There is the story of Moses, kept safely in a basket in the bulrushes. Baskets of early Egyptian origin show the same stitches we use today. In wealthy Roman homes there were baskets of elaborate design. The early Britons made their shields and huts of wickerwork, their boats of twigs woven and covered with skins. We learn of baskets thousands of years past in the Oriental world, of furniture woven long ago by the Chinese and Japanese as they weave furniture today.

But to the American Indian is due the credit for many of the useful basket forms and methods which we now employ in the United States. From the standpoint of design and beauty no one is a better artist than he, and in rhythmic techniques he is a past master. He wove most of his hunting and fishing equipment, as well as many useful objects—plaques, mats, snaring and fishing nets, grain bowls, and carrying baskets.

The first basket container may have been nothing more than a mesh of fibers drawn around a water gourd. The gourd made a valuable vessel to hold liquids, but it was very fragile; so the tribes-women learned to strengthen it by interlacing grasses and twigs around it. If the gourd broke nevertheless, its covering remained and became a useful basket.

Various arts owe their origin to basketry. From it sprang the

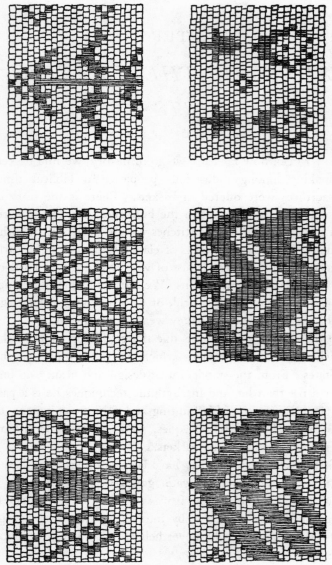

art of hand weaving and the fabrication of textiles. Coarse grasses, at first used whole for plaiting, were split into finer and finer strips until the finished woven material formed of them became flexible like cloth. These methods of interlacing were later used in weaving with soft, twisted strands of wool, flax, silk, and cotton.

Basketry is the beginning of pottery. Archaeologists say that basket forms were lined with clay for use in cooking; hot stones were dropped into these basket-pots to boil water. If too close a flame burned the basket away it also fired the clay, and thus by accident began the custom of using fired clay pots without their basket coverings.

Creative hand weaving as now practiced is applied to many different things—household baskets, trays, chair seats, wicker furniture, commercial baskets of all sizes and forms, clothesbaskets, measuring baskets, mats, and runners. In times of peace the markets of the world are well stocked with woven articles—Oriental, Scandinavian, English, Mexican, Indian, and those of many other nations—beautifully plaited fruit baskets, exquisite fiber mats, plaques, tea stands, doll furniture, hats, and novelties.

All these articles show the development of the weaving arts by men and women of various nationalities who, with skillful fingers, transformed the native fibers growing wild in their home lands. The Chinese, Indians, Mexicans, Aleutians, and even the Hottentots of South Africa, manifest great skill in weaving, incorporating their color schemes and design traditions into their work.

Neither in weaving nor basketry has the machine been able entirely to replace the fingers. We are therefore becoming more appreciative of the creative handwork developed through centuries of training in manual skills, and we are now eager to master these crafts for their own fascinating interest, for the useful goods they can supply, and for the industries they can create. Fortunately, we have fine examples of these in museums, and stories about them may be found in many books and records available in our libraries.

In connection with the use of this book, it will be profitable to delve into such other books as you may find in your community library, to study the hand-woven articles for sale in shops, and to visit museums with notebook and pencil. If you visit a museum, study the types, kinds, designs, and materials used in the woven objects of the Old World, as well as those devised by the American Indians. A community exhibit or program often brings out of homes valuable examples of woven products, baskets, and wicker furniture. There may be persons in your own neighbourhood who have both information and skills in many of the weaving crafts. These people may even have inherited and enjoyed certain valuable practices and efficient methods used in other countries, and are often pleased to co-operate with you in your work.

The Smithsonian Institution of Washington, D.C. and the Museum of Natural History of New York City, as well as museums in other cities, have large assortments of woven objects. A visit to any of these institutions will point up the historical importance of the woven products of the world, their unlimited technical range, and their beauty.

CHAPTER 2

WEAVING BY THE INDIANS

IT IS important to make sure that the best and most useful techniques in crafts practiced by the many tribes that once inhabited North America shall be conserved and made available for handicraft workers now and in the future. The American Indian weaver has not yet been surpassed in the beauty and design of his product.

The actual weaving of Indian products was done by the squaw, using whatever material she could find at hand—simple grasses, split bark, or even twigs. Her colors were the dull browns and blues of the sun-baked prairies, the creamy yellow of willow tops growing near springs, the reddish brown of the redbud bark, the glossy black from the stem of the maidenhair fern. For still more variety of color she prepared vegetable dyes that deepened and grew mellow with age. Great pride in her work and infinite patience were the admirable qualities of this craftswoman. She experimented with new materials, dyes, and weaves. We trace tribal connections today through basketry stitches and borders the tribeswomen wove; similar workmanship shows cultural connection between the tribes who made them.

To the Indian, the interweaving of fibers represented many arts. Woven into each product is tradition, folklore, history, poetry, art, and religion. The life of nature is a part of Indians' designs— streams and trees, animals and birds, often in conventional form. In museums the world over, the variety, utility, beauty, and quantity of Indian-woven articles impress the observer. These exhibits illustrate the fact that the various Indian tribes have had great skill

7

in hand crafts. They have combined substantiality and rare art in the production of a wide variety of articles: water bottles, grain bowls, sacred plaques, dance baskets, practical utensils, fishing and hunting nets, and baskets in which to carry children.

Modern industry and merchandise have well-nigh killed this creative activity of the American Indian. The squaw, for instance, no longer cherishes her homemade basket. For a few cents she can buy pots and pans in which to do her cooking. Though basket-making is still practiced in some tribes, few use baskets as their ancestors did. Often the Indian of the western United States works for the commercial trade, making mats or baskets of sweet grass or splints. While these are well woven, they lack the beauty of design characteristic of the individual worker who creates from a deep love of his craft and a desire to express himself in its forms.

THREE BASKETS OF THE AMERICAN INDIAN
A square-shaped basket of paired cattails and cedar bark *(upper right);*
a handy catchall basket of flat cane decorated with bird feathers *(upper left),*
and a basket of flat reed in two colors *(below).*

MOTIFS FOUND IN INDIAN WOVEN DESIGNS

Designs, too, are often taken from non-Indian sources. Our civilization, for its own benefit, should encourage each new generation of Indians to learn and to perpetuate their weaving skills, and should make it possible for others—young and old—to learn the fascinating techniques.

TYPICAL INDIAN DESIGNS AND FORMS

The outstanding achievement of the American Indians in weaving was their gift for original and elaborate design. Their

CONVENTIONALIZED DESIGN TREATMENT GIVEN TO NATURAL OBJECTS

methods and products have therefore been of great interest to artists and collectors. Indian baskets and rugs owe much of their charm to a woven texture of clever geometric or artistic patterns. There are three distinct types of weaves known as *checkerwork*, *wickerwork*, and *twilling*. These designs, used in the weaving of both baskets and fabrics, were also employed in Indian pottery and clay modeling.

Just as the different tribes reveal their characteristics and history in decorative design, and maintain their own traditions of design and symbolism, so do their various products—trays, buckets, bowls, and plaques—express in an interesting way the daily habits and industrial usages of their makers. The craftsman of today should seek to become familiar with these types and forms as a background to his own creative work. This study may also be made with a view to determining why in some localities certain types and forms have been maintained, and found more or less permanently useful to the civilization which inspired them. For instance, one of the most distinctive styles of North American weaving is that evolved by the Indians of the coast and mountain regions of southern California, the so-called Mission tribes. The Mission weavers used three materials in their work: a local grass for the foundation and either sumac or rush for wrapping weaves. They did not seem to care for some materials—yucca, willow twigs, or long pine needles—used by neighboring peoples. One reason for their restricted use of materials may have been that their products were generally burden vessels, such as water and food containers, which must be tightly woven and resistant to wear.

Color in Mission designs was achieved by introducing juncus rush, which grows in a great variety of hues and shades. The color and design of Mission products was always pleasing, adhering to a mottled or geometric plan. The only pictures used were of snakes, birds, human beings, and simple objects of nature.

The domestic vessels of Indian design are useful in our civilized domestic settings. The homemaker of today finds the ancient grain basket just right in shape for many uses—for fruit bowl, yarn basket, or wastebasket; the ceremonial plaques are perfect for bread trays or cake holders; the half-cylindrical shapes which were devised for carrying, are easily convertible to fishing kits or pack baskets.

CHAPTER 3

PREPARATION FOR WORK

THE SUCCESS of craft work, like success in other things, is dependent largely upon plans and preparations made in advance. To make plans, the craftsman must be familiar with the kinds of raw materials he will use; he must understand terms and their definitions in order to follow directions; and he must select his supplies and arrange to get them before work can begin. He will need some knowledge of the various forms, shapes, and sizes of articles his craft can produce. He should know how to keep his tools in good condition and how properly to prepare materials in order to insure their best condition and his own convenience while working with them.

CRAFT MATERIALS

There is an abundance of materials, both natural and manufactured, available for crafts. Educational supply companies in various large cities offer reliable raw materials. Many fibers of local origin may be just as successfully used for weaving purposes as some of these commercial products, but in order to be ready for use, they must be gathered at the right time, cured, and treated. You can weave with grasses, mosses, vines, stems, leaves, pine needles, cornhusks, cane, and even with strips of bark properly gathered and seasoned. You can use twine or twisted paper.*

---

* Information regarding the gathering and preparation of over 100 kinds of native materials for basketmaking found in the United States is given in the book *Basket Pioneering*, Creative Crafts, East Berlin, Pa.

In addition to knowing how to prepare these various materials the craft worker should be familiar with sources of helpful aid and information. Individuals in your own neighborhood may be experts in making some particular article or handling some interesting material. Find out who they are and seek their guidance and help. The public library, magazine files, catalogues, local stores, and factories may also furnish a variety of information.

WEAVING TOOLS AND THEIR CARE

The tools necessary for efficient workmanship are simple and inexpensive. Plan to own as many as you can of the essential ones, some of which are illustrated here. With the initial equipment listed you will be ready to use your free moments advantageously and to fill your leisure time with pleasant and profitable enterprise. Here is your list:

Ruler	Hammer
Notebook	Awl
Sharp scissors	Pliers
Sloyd knife	Saw
Tapeline	Sandpaper
Pencils and crayons	Wiping cloth

Keep your tools in good condition. They should be sharp, clean, and placed in order. A tool case or kit aids greatly in systematizing the care of tools, or they may be kept in the pocket of your work apron. Tool kits can be made of leather, wood, or fiber.

WORK AND STORAGE SPACE

A well-lighted and well-ventilated room is desirable for any pleasant activity. The table or desk space required for basket or fiber weaving is about the same as that required for writing, study, or sewing. You can operate with greater efficiency and satisfaction when you have enough table space to give you perfect freedom in handling materials and equipment. Desks or tables should be covered and protected with heavy paper or oilcloth. They should be suited to individual needs and projects. You will find it convenient and restful to have several tables of different heights, if possible, so that you can stand during some processes and be seated during others.

Sufficient storage space should be provided for the mass of material necessary. When craft groups are working in one place, space should be provided for the storing of all half-finished work and material, preferably in a separate room with plenty of shelving.

PROTECTION WHILE WORKING

A simple apron of heavy cloth or rubber will be required. For a durable, practical protector that has been found serviceable for the purpose, see Chapter 4. Place as many of your tools and materials as possible in the pockets of the apron.

When ready for work, arrange your tools in order on the work table. Have everything where you can reach it the instant you need it for the successive steps of the work. Weaving well done is a rhythmic process, and both pleasure and efficiency are spoiled if the rhythm must be broken to hunt for tools or materials in a disorderly work place.

STAINING, PAINTING, OR WAXING

After a product is completed, considerable beauty of appearance can be given to it by staining, painting, or waxing. It is important to know beforehand about the possibilities of such finishes. The kind to use depends upon the nature of the article and the preference of the worker. Some people who like the natural color of native material prefer a shellac finish; others like to stain objects a darker tone, waxed, perhaps, to a smooth polish that feels soft and velvety to the touch; others think that a coat of paint adds attractiveness. Before you paint or stain your product, it is a good idea to consult someone who understands such matters, perhaps inviting him to your home or workshop for a demonstration. Practical painters, art teachers, and decorators are usually available and are glad to respond to such invitations. Drawing, art, and vocational teachers may be invited to co-operate with any class or group.

SUGGESTIONS FOR THE WORKER

Start at the bottom and progress by easy steps until you can build one piece well. Keep practicing until you can rely on obtaining a uniform pleasing shape. Most native materials are strong and durable, and can be used and re-used for practice work.

Learn to make pencil sketches and outlines for your guidance. Know what you are trying to accomplish—then go patiently to your goal. Occasionally we all get tired and discouraged, and are tempted to stop before we complete what we set out to make. One of the basic principles of craft work is the artistic completion of every object planned; leaving a job unfinished limits the creative experience.

PLANNING AND PREPARATION

To avoid the dissatisfactions that result from unfinished work calls for planning before a project is undertaken. The teacher or leader of a craft group soon learns to consider projects with reference to the abilities, needs, and circumstances of the individuals who must execute them. The individual who works without a teacher must give the same sort of consideration, informally at least, to his own projects.

Among the first considerations is the level of the worker's talent and interest. Can he carry to successful completion the project he undertakes; does he have or can he develop the skills and abilities

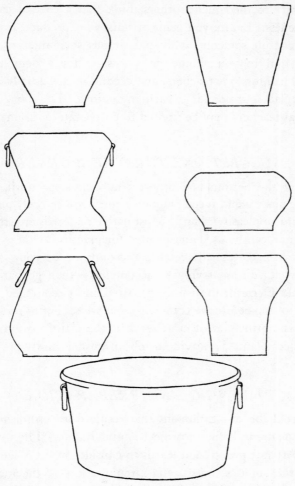

OUTLINES FOR UTILITARIAN BASKET FORMS

to do the work needed? Will he enjoy the project, either at its beginning or as he gets further into it?

If he knows what he wants to do, and can start it with good hope of carrying through, still other things remain to be considered:

1. Can he afford the time and materials?
2. Can the materials be obtained?
3. Can he use, enjoy, or dispose of what he plans to make?

The self-taught weaver should learn to understand and guide himself just as the teacher-leader analyzes and guides his followers. The overambitious should not be allowed to encounter disappoint-

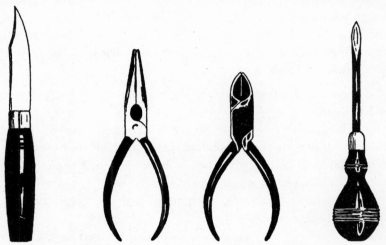

A KNIFE, PINCERS, SPOKE OR WIRE CUTTER, AND AWL NEEDLE
ARE NECESSITIES IN ALL FIBER WEAVING

ment, yet their imagination and interest must be stimulated. Some beginning weavers may not have seen enough woven-fiber work to rouse them to enthusiasm. Such persons may go alone or in small parties to visit museums, libraries, exhibits, stores, factories, and even private homes where materials, procedures, and finished work can be seen. The things seen will start creative ideas.

An interested individual will keep himself busy searching for fresh ideas and plans for projects, and an enthusiastic class will be a challenge to the teacher's resourcefulness. Either learner or teacher will want to make the most of observation trips. On such trips, therefore, look for sources of help, information, and inspiration; seek experts from whom you may secure instruction in special lines, and keep in touch with them; note names and uses of new materials and products; note new designs, patterns, and plans for doing your work; be alert for ideas for marketing your products, and find the best methods of advertising and display of finished goods.

On your trips carry a notebook, a sketchbook, a fountain pen, and a tapeline for measuring. If your notes are made with pencil, copy them later with ink into a permanent book. Classify your notes under headings such as:

1. Sources of information: books, magazines, reports (printed), and bulletins.

2. Guidance by experts: names, addresses, and telephone numbers of experts you locate, and work in which they excel.

3. Materials discovered; where they can be found or purchased.

4. Exhibits, and products shown in each.

5. Designs and patterns, with measurements, color schemes, finish, and other details.

6. Marketing: buyers, prices, methods of advertising, and all related information.

CHAPTER 4

PROTECTOR OR WORK APRON

A PERSON IS well dressed when appropriately dressed for his work. The weaving worker is no exception. He needs a work apron as a protector for other clothing, as a convenience for a handy arrangement of small materials and tools while at work, and as a case for keeping them together between work periods.

Work aprons are best made of a durable, strong material such as denim or colored cotton cloth. These come in tan, brown, blue, gray, and other shades. Exhibition aprons to wear at sales or showings may be of white cotton or rayon. Ties at the neck and waist may be made of the same cloth, or of binding tape, or of shoe laces. Good sewing materials should be used. A large needle is best for the basting, and strong scissors for cutting the heavy cloth. For the final stitching, machine sewing is best.

An apron for a small adult or a child of ten to fourteen requires a piece of cloth about 24 inches wide and 30 inches long. The cloth for a full-size apron should be about 26 to 30 inches wide and 36 inches long. The length is governed by the height of the wearer and by the amount of cloth used for turning up into pockets and hems. These dimensions may be accurately determined by the use of a paper pattern and a tape measure.

The following picture shows the sheet of cloth with the upper corners turned down to form the bib of the apron. The lines at the bottom indicate the approximate position, size, and number of the pockets to be used for larger tools and for materials; the approximate depth of the necessary fold in the cloth is shown.

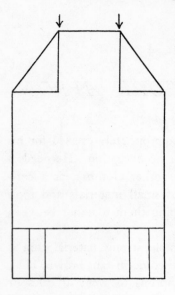

The picture below gives an idea of the appearance of a finished apron, with the tools and materials in place. Note the use of the turned-down corners for bib pockets. Compare the position of the lower pockets with the hem position suggested in the upper picture. These alternative positions depend on the wearer's preference. Being weighted by the tools, the hem-pocket apron tends to hang fully extended when the wearer stands at his work; but when he sits down, the pockets may be drawn up over his knees, to prevent the contents

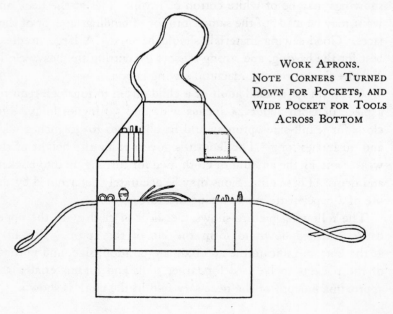

WORK APRONS.
NOTE CORNERS TURNED
DOWN FOR POCKETS, AND
WIDE POCKET FOR TOOLS
ACROSS BOTTOM

from spilling. The high pockets remain vertical in either sitting or standing position. These high pockets are made by sewing an 8- or 10-inch strip of cloth at whatever height the wearer desires. This high-pocket design has a further advantage over the hem-pocket design; the apron can be made as long as the wearer desires, even ankle length.

When fiber-weaving projects are carried on as group activity in clubs or schools, every member of the group should have a work apron. He should also have a place to store the apron, materials, and tools between work periods. Such storage may be a locker or shelf near the work place, or a bag, box, or case to be carried home. If the weaving worker contemplates home projects between meetings, such a carrier is absolutely necessary.

School credit in sewing or manual training classes can often be given to students who make their own carrying bags or boxes.

PART II

Basketmaking

CHAPTER 5

BASKETMAKING FUNDAMENTALS

ASKETRY IS a delightful craft that requires no expensive
equipment, yet produces very useful and salable articles.
The rhythm of the work is fascinating. Problems of
creating symmetrical forms and of adding original touches of
design render the work doubly fascinating. And a skilled basket
worker can earn money by selling his products or by organizing
groups and teaching them.

MATERIALS

The materials most familiar and available to both new and
experienced basketweavers are reed, rattan, raffia, and the commercial cords and twines. Supply houses have these materials at
reasonable prices. Native twigs, vines, grasses, pine needles, cornhusks, rushes, and cattails are excellent and are obtainable in many
localities. Basketry materials are usually flexible and serviceable
over long periods. A basket several years old can be unraveled and
the fibers used again for a new basket.

WORKROOM

The first essential for work is ample space, indoors or out. If
indoors, choose a well-lighted room. In summertime a cool, convenient place to work is a basement where water is available, or a
shaded porch or garden. A group of Girl Scouts once adopted a

niche of woodland by the bridge of a stream where they could sit on the rocks and dip their baskets in the water around them. (See frontispiece.) A near-by tent was used on rainy days.

PREPARATION FOR WORK

Basket reed comes in long skeins and, like most basketry materials, is often dry and brittle, requiring soaking in water. Remove one reed at a time from the bundle, always drawing from the loop end. Roll each reed into a coil for soaking, fastening its end by twisting several times around the coil; or take several reeds in a group and wrap into small bundles for convenience in future storage and soaking. Reed substitutes may be wound into coils, but they do not require soaking.

Heavy reed materials used for spokes and handles should be cut into lengths measured according to the needs of the product being made. Let the reed soak in water ten or fifteen minutes, or until pliable, and use while damp and flexible. You can keep the reed moist by wrapping it in a wet bath towel or a gunny sack. If the reed dries out, place it in water again for a short time.

The sizes of reed produced by basketry supply houses are fairly uniform and standard. Slight deviations may be adjusted, and in cases where native materials are used, it is possible to make an accurate comparison of these with the sizes sold commercially. Examine the chart of sizes on pages 27–29.

For making basket handles, Nos. 6 and 7 are used, with smaller reed for the wrapping.

For spokes and bi-spokes, Nos. 3, 4, and 5 are generally used.

For weavers in small or medium-size baskets, Nos. 2 and 3 are used; in large baskets (firewood baskets, wastebaskets, and the like) the larger reeds, Nos. 4 to 7, are needed.

TOOLS

In Chapter 3 there is a list of tools needed for hand weaving in general (see page 13 and page 17). Basketweaving calls for certain additional tools:

Winding awl   Rubber finger guard   Pincers
Sponge   Glass jar   Dishpan (for soaking reeds)

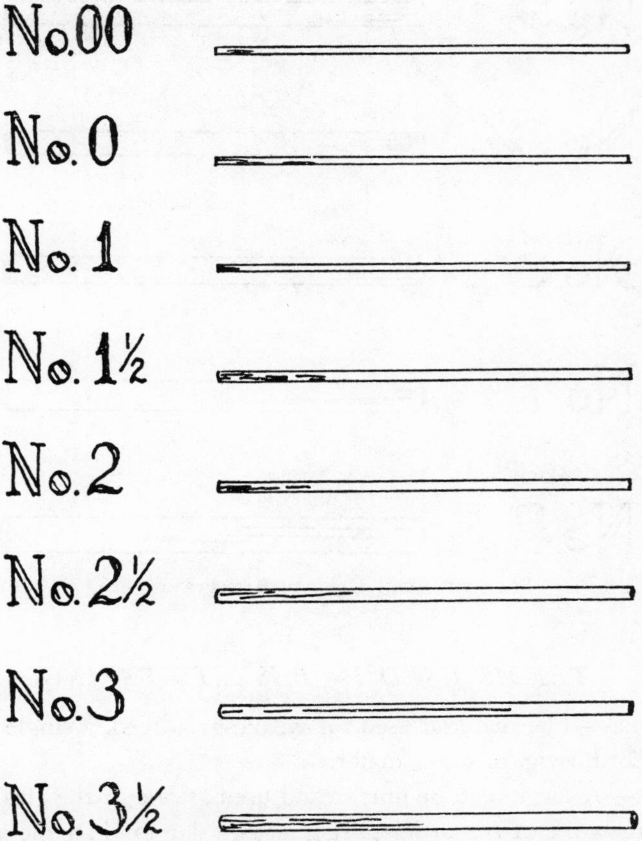

No.00

No. 0

No. 1

No. 1½

No. 2

No. 2½

No. 3

No. 3½

Sizes of Reed Used in Basketry (see also pages 28 and 29)

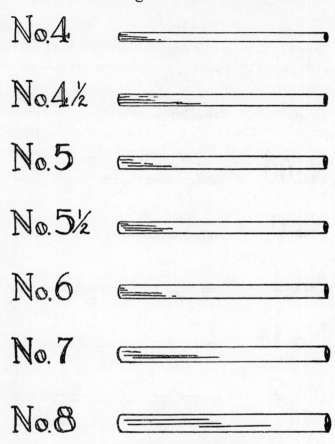

No.4

No.4½

No.5

No.5½

No.6

No.7

No.8

SIZES OF REED USED IN BASKETRY (*cont.*)

TERMS USED IN BASKETWEAVING

WEAVER—The material used for weaving: a reed, a single strand of cord, twig, or other material.

SPOKE—A large reed or unit strand used as one of the ribs of the framework of the article. It is usually larger than the weaver strands. Wire spokes are sometimes used as a foundation with

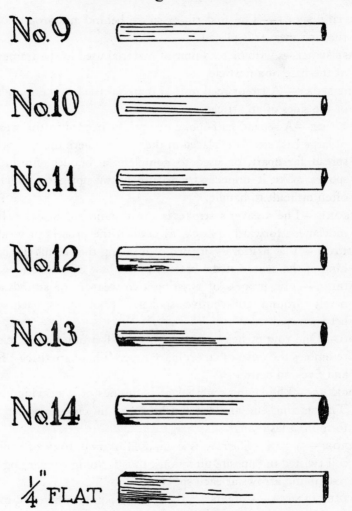

No. 9

No. 10

No. 11

No. 12

No. 13

No. 14

¼″ FLAT

SIZES OF REED USED IN BASKETRY (*cont.*)

reed substitutes, the advantage being that the wire spokes do not need soaking. This process might ruin a fiber cord, which is made of paper.

INITIAL SPOKE—The first rib or spoke behind and around which the first weaver is placed.

BASE SPOKE—A rib or reed unit of material used in the framework of the base of an article.

SIDE SPOKE—A rib or reed unit of material used in the foundation of the sides of an article.

BI-SPOKE—A second half-spoke or upright needed in the weaving of large baskets. It is placed in the spaces where the spokes have spread far apart, or used to complete a braided finish. Bi-spokes make it unnecessary to use heavy uprights, which are often difficult to handle.

STROKE—The weaver's stroke is the distance of a single hand-movement forward or back, as used in the process of weaving.

BUTTON—The first cross or turn of weaving that forms the beginning of the center of the bottom of the base of a basket.

PAIRING—The process of twisting two weavers or strands alternately around consecutive spokes. They cross each other between spokes.

COIL—One row of heavy weaving made all around an article. It resembles the twist of an ordinary rope. There are three-, four-, and five-rod coils.

LOCKING—The laying together of both ends of a weaving strand. The starting end and the finishing end lie close together, thus forming a fastening.

ARROW—A row of arrow is composed of two rows of ordinary coil twisted in opposite directions, thus forming converging lines resembling arrows at each spoke.

BASKET CENTER—Centers are the starting points of all oval, round, or oblong articles with woven bases. Centers are referred to by names based upon their origin and history. The principal types are: *Moki centers,* created and used by the Moki Indians; *Italian centers,* which originated in Italy and have been used by the gypsy basketweavers ever since their early history; *Japanese*

TWIST OF RATTAN

CUT
←STRING
HERE

A TWIST OF RATTAN AS IT COMES FROM THE SHOP

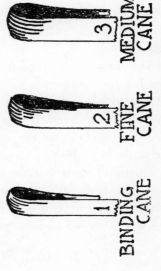

BINDING CANE 1   FINE CANE 2   MEDIUM CANE 3

SIZES OF CANE USED FOR SEATING

31

centers, which are useful in starting baskets with one weaver. There are also other types of centers, which will be described later.

BASKET BASE—The part of the basket that rests horizontally on floor or table. In a hanging basket it is the lowest portion, where the spokes are first laid together and the weavers start interlacing them.

BASKET SIDES—The sides of a basket are the parts that rise upwards from the base.

BASKET BORDER—The edge added to finish off spokes at top or bottom of basket, made by twisting the spokes around one another.

BASKET SHOULDER—The shoulder of a basket is its turn at the top, which is a rounded curve.

BASKET HANDLE—The portion by which the basket is held. Handles may be decorative, hanging at the sides of the basket, or they may go over the top, extending above it.

BASKET LID—Some baskets have lids or covers. A cover may be flat, dome shaped, or inverted like a saucer.

PIECING—The addition of a new weaver to replace the old when the latter comes to its end. Piecing is usually done behind the spoke where the old weaver ended.

WORKING SUGGESTIONS

1. To insure greater rigidity and better form, work with spokes, bi-spokes, and uprights without soaking them. The ends, however, must always be soaked before binding the base or weaving the border.

2. Reed weavers should always be soaked before using, and re-soaked if they have been allowed to stand and dry out.

3. Keep all tools and materials in a permanent and well-organized place. Nothing will defeat your progress more than losing or misplacing equipment.

4. The rule in weaving is to weave from left to right. Always start under the first spoke and over the second, and weave from the inside to the outside, except in tray weaving. In this case, it is often desirable to weave from the outside to the inside, as this practice leaves the ends of the weavers inside and protected.

5. To follow a well-defined procedure, study the text and know:

> Materials and where to get them.
> Tools needed and how to use them.
> Basic weaves and how they are made.
> Kinds of bases and how they are made.
> How to make the transition between the base and sides of a basket.
> How base borders are made.
> How top or finishing borders are made.
> Kinds of handles, and methods of making them.
> How to finish, true up, trim, and shape a product.
> Stains, paints, and dyes used, and how to apply them.
> How to vary instructions to make an article larger or smaller; how to modify instructions to change the form of an article.
> How to mend spokes, weavers, and handles; and how to alter bases, sides, and borders.

When you have mastered the preceding fundamentals, it will be easy to advance rapidly, as practice will be your chief requisite.

6. Avoid progressing too quickly. Study the groundwork and master it before trying more advanced projects. It is a mistake to rush forward, attempting many difficult products before the basic principles are understood.

7. Let the making of gifts in connection with the work be a special challenge. No finer gifts can be made than articles created by skilled hands and inspired by a generous heart.

8. Choose suitable lining materials for baskets that need padding.

Sewing baskets need plain, durable linings with pockets, partitions, and compartments for specific uses. Jewelry and candy baskets should have inner trimmings with dainty colors for an artistic effect. Scrap baskets, market and laundry baskets may be lined with simple, washable or waterproof cloth, which should be so fastened that it can easily be removed and replaced.

9. It is necessary to learn the use of bi-spokes, or seconds. Without this second, or bi-spoke, it would be necessary to add a complete spoke, which would crowd the stitches and affect the appearance of the basket.

10. When weaving with canes, rushes, bull pines, willow twigs, and grasses, follow the same instructions as given for weaving with reed; but make allowances for the width of weavers in determining the numbers of rows of weaving necessary to complete the article. Pine needles and grasses are used in clumps, the weaving worker making each clump as large as desired. This process is described in detail later. Raffia is used to stitch the rows together.

11. A teacher planning an advanced course in creative weaving should start his pupils making articles similar to those in this textbook, but with variations in weave, design, shape, and size. From these simple patterns they can progress to advanced projects such as boxes, with inner linings and trimmings, for candy, collars, and jewelry, as well as doll cradles, desk sets, picture frames, foot rests, fireplace baskets, porch lamps, floor and table lamps, ferneries, and furniture for home, room, and office.

CHAPTER 6

BASKET BASES AND HOW TO WEAVE THEM

T HE BASE is the starting point in the weaving of a basket. A good basket is built on a firm, well-woven base. Mastery of the methods of base weaving is therefore a vital point in the success of all basketweaving.

At the center of the base is the small, round, hard place where the spokes cross and where they should be first tied together. This is called the *button*. Radiating from it, the spokes extend outward in groups. The Pairing Weave is used to gradually separate the spokes and to make them equidistant. After this is accomplished, any suitable weaving stitch may be used to continue around the spokes.

DIFFERENCES IN CONSTRUCTION

In general, bases may be divided into two groups:

First, those bases in which the spokes are cut long enough for the weaving of the entire base and for turning up for the weaving of the sides, or even for completing the entire basket.

Second, those bases in which the base spokes are cut to make the base only, and extra spokes are added for the sides. Here the spokes of the base are planned and cut in either of two ways: (*a*) If not too stiff, they are cut long enough to extend about $1\frac{1}{2}$ inches into the basket sides. The additional spokes, long enough for the sides, are added by inserting one new side spoke at the left of each end of the base spokes. This practice gives the same number of spokes for the sides as for the base. The weaving is continued over the

35

old end and the new spoke as if they were one, until the old end gives out. You then continue with the new spoke only. If more spokes are desired, insert one each beside every new spoke. If at any time the spokes seem too close for weaving, clip off every second spoke. (*b*) If the spokes are thick and not easily bent, they are clipped off after the new spokes have been added. Then two new spokes may be added, one on each side of each stiff base spoke (page 37, Sketch *E*).

MAKING BASES

1. All spokes must radiate from the exact center of the base and must be equidistant from each other. This formation comes about gradually by the sinking down of the weaver between the spokes.

2. All weaving must be performed with the same tension. Keep the weavers close together. Pull on each one at the same point in the process and with the same strength of hand.

3. The curve of the base should be like an inverted saucer. To produce this effect, curve the spokes evenly downward. Continue the even, strong pull on each weaver in succession to maintain this curve. In a 5-inch base the center should be about $\frac{1}{2}$ inch up off the table, with only the outside edges of the base resting upon it.

4. In turning up the base spokes, or the newly inserted side spokes, soak the spokes first until pliable, and then pinch each spoke with pincers at its bending point. This treatment softens the fibers so that they will bend without breaking.

5. Practice making bases until you can produce a perfect one, rounding out its shape into a domelike saucer form (page 37, Sketch *G*).

THREE TYPES OF BASES

Use the following directions for starting three typical and useful styles of basket bases: (1) the Japanese base; (2) the simple

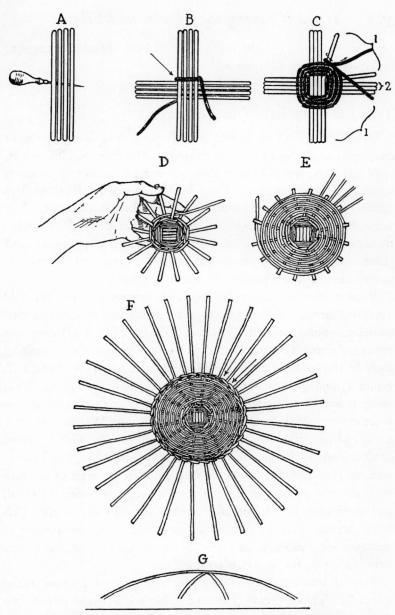

VARIOUS STEPS IN THE MAKING OF A JAPANESE BASE

eight-spoke base; (3) the Indian basket base. (For references to basket-weaves, see Chapter 8.)

THE JAPANESE BASE (*sketches, page* 37)

Use eight spokes of desired size, Nos. 3 or 4 being the most frequently used. Split four of these spokes at their centers (Sketch *A*, page 37), then pass the other four spokes through the split spokes, known as *threading* the spokes. To thread easily, place the four spokes on a block of wood while you pierce them with an awl. Lay these four spokes side by side, then slip the other four spokes through the groove thus made. Hold the eight spokes in both hands and curve them downward from the center in the saucer-shaped curve. Then proceed to weave as follows:

Bend a No. 2 weaver double at its center, and lay the fold around a group of four spokes (Sketch *B*, arrow). Make two complete rounds with the Pairing Weave (Sketch *C*) over the groups of four. Then divide the spokes into groups of two, making pairs of the spokes which are adjacent at the corners (Sketch *C*, group 1) and the two spokes left between them (group 2). Push weavers well down between them. Gradually this spaces the spokes more evenly. Make two more rounds of Pairing Weave over these groups of two, then separate the spokes into singles with a pairing stitch around each separate spoke. At this point change to a larger weaver, No. 3, and continue to weave out to the edge of the base with the one weaver, going over two spokes and under the third, and continuing thus round after round (Sketches *D* and *E*). This is the Japanese Weave. It can be used only when the number of spokes is *not* a multiple of three. Since the number of spoke-ends here is sixteen, this weave is possible.

For the last round at the very edge or outside of the base, make a round of Triple Weave (Sketch *F*). Now insert new spokes, one at the left of each old base spoke (Sketch *F*, arrows) and prepare to weave the sides. If base spokes are too stiff for sides, insert two spokes at each old spoke, one at either side, and trim off the old spokes flush with the base (Sketch *E*).

The Japanese Base may start with sets of five instead of four spokes. The weaving stitch may be changed to Pairing after the spokes have been divided. By a change of stitch, interesting texture effects are obtained.

THE SIMPLE EIGHT-SPOKE BASE (*sketches, below*)

Choose eight spokes of desired size. Pierce four at their centers with an awl and insert the other four through the slits, just as was

A   **B**

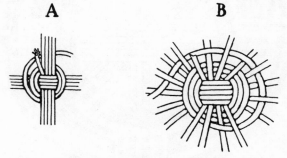

STARTING AND CONTINUING SIMPLE BASKET BASE

done for Japanese base (page 37). Start a single weaver of No. 2 reed by inserting it at a corner (*above*, Sketch *A*). Pass the weaver under and over the groups of four spokes for three rounds. Now cut out one spoke. Cutting it out leaves an uneven number of spokes and makes it possible to weave around them with Under-and-Over Weave with the one weaver, as shown. The rows alternate with each other. Gradually make the base a saucer shape. Change to Pairing Weave if desired. Finish the edge with a row of Pairing or Triple Weave (Chapter 8). *B* above shows an uneven number of spokes.

THE INDIAN BASKET BASE (*sketches, below and page* 41)

In making the Indian center, sixteen spokes are required. They are used in sets of four in making the button. Locate the exact center of each set. Hold the first set horizontally. The second set should be placed in a vertical position back of the first set of four.

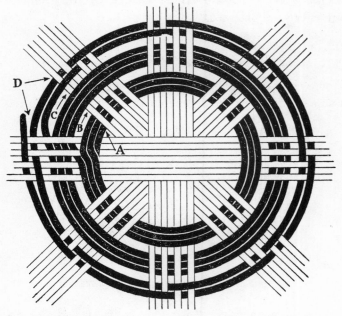

STEPS IN MAKING THE INDIAN BASKET BASE (see also next page)

The third set is placed diagonally back of the first two, running from right to left. The fourth set is placed diagonally behind the other three, running from left to right. Now, by holding all four sets in position, you are ready to weave by starting a No. 2 weaver behind the left diagonal set (*A, above*). Now pass the weaver through the center of a set of four and bring it up and over the sets of spokes that it went under before, and under those it went over (as shown at *B*). Make three more rounds.

Now separate the sets of four into pairs, and continue by weaving under and over the pairs (as at *C*). At the end of the first round, pass under two successive pairs (indicated by arrows at *D*), which will again bring the weaver over the pairs it went under in previous

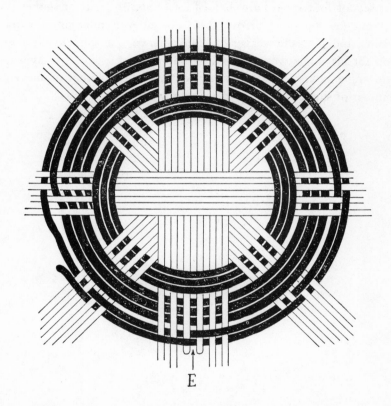

E

row, and under those it went over. The single weaver can be used provided this process is repeated in each round; it may be still better to cut out a pair of spokes to give an uneven number of pairs, after which the single weaver will automatically alternate.

It is also possible to keep an even number of pairs of spokes and use a second weaver; if the rounds are made first with one weaver and then with the other, each row will alternate with the one preceding it.

This same type of base may be made with more spokes (*E*, page 41). Here the second set is composed of six spokes, and after the sets of four spokes are divided into two, one pair of spokes is cut out (as shown at arrow, *E*). An uneven number of pairs results, and gives the weaver the convenience of automatic alternation for his single weaver. If later the pairs of spokes are divided into single spokes, one spoke can be cut out, thus making an uneven number of single spokes for the single weaver.

CHAPTER 7

THE OVAL BASE

O VAL BASES are used for market baskets, clothesbaskets, fishing baskets, and oval trays. They are not difficult to construct; the shape is pleasing and the type of base very useful. In an oval base a core of initial spokes runs through the long center, and is crossed by cross-spokes or needles, like so many legs of a centipede.

STEPS IN CONSTRUCTION

BINDING THE CROSS-SPOKES TO THE CENTRAL CORE (*sketch, page* 44)

Cut the group of three or five initial spokes (threads) that are to form the core, of fairly large reed and just a little longer than you plan for the finished base. These are not bent upward; auxiliary spokes are inserted at the edge of the base. The cross-spokes (needles) are of the same size or one size smaller. Slit these needles at their centers, as shown in small sketch, and slip the long initial spokes through two of these at a time. Bind each two cross-spokes in place before adding the next two.

MAKING THE BINDING CROSS (*sketch, page* 44)

To make the cross shown at each intersection, use a well-soaked strand of No. 2 or No. 3 reed. Insert this through the slits of the needles as shown. Pinch the weaving strand at the points of bending, to prevent breaking. Follow the directions of arrows,

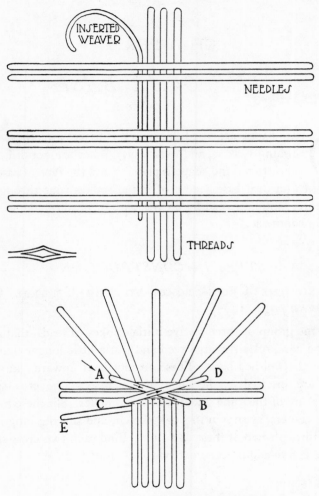

FIRST STEPS IN WEAVING OVAL BASE

proceeding in order from start of weaver at *A*, to *B*, under the threads, then to *C*, *D*, and under the cross to *E*.

Between the binding crosses, wrap the weaver around the

initial spokes, making eight turns or so (*sketch, below*). Then add the next pair of needles, bind these to the thread-spokes with the cross, and wrap the weaver around the threads eight more

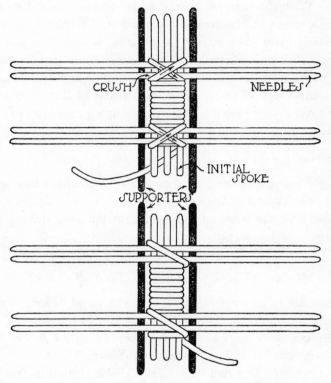

STEPS IN WRAPPING CORE OF OVAL BASE

times. Continue this until you add the last pair of needles, at the same distance from its end of the spokes as first pair is from its end.

Add side supports of heavy reed to central core if necessary. These supports are shown by heavy lines (*above*). The underside of the section is shown in the same illustration.

WEAVING AROUND OVAL FRAME

To weave, simply continue with the flexible weaver that made the crosses. Weave all around oval frame, under and over the spokes. With the even number of spokes you will need two alternating weavers in the weave described in Chapter 8 as Single Under-and-Over Weave, using alternating weavers. If you wish to work with one weaver only, either cut out a spoke or add a bi-spoke from center to one side. For almost any oval base, use Under-and-Over Weave; either the Pairing or Triple Weave is apt to twist a long base out of shape, though a few rows of either may be used.

TURNING UP SIDES

Simply insert a spoke on either side of each main base spoke. Use Triple Weave at the edge to finish the base. Squeeze each new spoke at the point of bending, turn upward, and continue weaving.

MAKING AN OVAL CLOTHESBASKET

There are other ways in which to start an oval basket. Two of these are shown on page 47.

First cut three or five thread-spokes 10 to 12 inches long. Cross with needles 8 to 10 inches long (Sketch 1).

First method: Use two well-soaked pliable strands of No. 2 or No. 3 reed, and make a round of Pairing Weave (Sketch 2). This fastens the spoke in place. After eight to ten rounds of Pairing, change to Under-and-Over Weave (Sketch 6). Add one spoke to make an uneven number for weaving the remainder of base with Under-and-Over Weave, using one weaver.

Second method: Use two weaving strands of No. 2 or No. 3 reed, or a single strand doubled at center. In Sketch 3 one strand is shown light, the other dark. Weave first with one end, then with

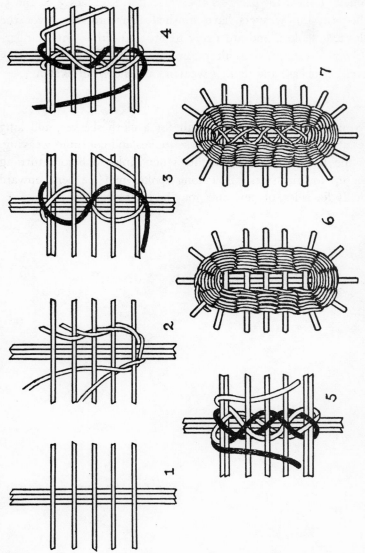

VARIOUS STEPS IN WEAVING THE BOTTOM OF A CLOTHESBASKET

the other. Follow the progress of each reed in Sketches 3, 4, and 5. In the last, the weavers have finished their crossings over the needles and spokes, and are ready to proceed either with Under-and-Over Weave, using alternating weavers, or with Pairing Weave. This base and its first weaving are shown in Sketch 7.

Enlarging the Base

To make the base large enough for a clothesbasket, add long spokes at either side of the first base spokes and continue weaving. Press the base flat under weights when finished before turning spokes up for the sides. The long spokes may be bent upward gradually for sides, or new ones may be inserted.

CHAPTER 8

BASIC WEAVES AND DIREC-
TIONS FOR MAKING THEM

THE NAMES of the different weaves are, in most instances, based upon the number of reeds used, the direction of the strands in weaving, and the relative position of the weaving reed in the processes of weaving. The important weaves are:

1. Single Under-and-Over Weave
2. Double Under-and-Over Weave
3. Single Japanese Weave
4. Double Japanese Weave
5. Twill Weave
6. Colonial Weave
7. Bellefonte Weave
8. Band Weave
9. Pairing Weave
10. Double Pairing Weave
11. Triple Weave
12. Coil Weave
13. Arrow Weave

PREPARATION AND PRACTICING

Have weavers ready for use; soak these in tepid water before using. If spokes are brittle, wet them for a half hour; otherwise, for a few minutes. Work with wet or moist hands.

Have clearly in mind the size, form, and specifications of objects to be made.

Prepare a sketch and determine these dimensions: (*a*) diameter of base; (*b*) height of basket; (*c*) diameter of inside opening from rim to rim; (*d*) greatest diameter from side to side.

Select and follow the diagrams of the weaves to be employed.

Remember that the weaving always goes from left to right, except at the beginning (for example, when fastening uprights below the base of a tray, then weave from right to left).

Practice the weaving of bases, making several kinds, before attempting the side weaves. The base is the foundation and the sides are built up from it. Also practice the transition between the base and sides (page 37, Sketches *E*, *F*).

Never be satisfied with your first base; use it for practice work only. Undo your first attempts, resoak the reed in tepid water, and use the same reed again for the weaving of a more perfect base. Then begin the weaving of the sides. Master the basic weaves one at a time.

UNDER-AND-OVER-WEAVES

SINGLE UNDER-AND-OVER WEAVE (*pages 51 and 52, Sketch* 1)

(*a*) *If a single weaver is used,* an odd number of spokes is required. Start the weaver behind a spoke near base or beginning point. Then carry weaver in front of next spoke and weave around basket, passing under and over successive spokes until the article is complete and ready for rim and handles.

(*b*) *If two weavers are used,* one alternating with the other, an even number of spokes is required. Take the first weaver around basket and back to starting point before you use the second weaver. Insert second weaver behind the spoke next at right of first spoke and carry this around basket, alternating with position of first weaver; that is, *back* of each spoke that first weaver went *over*. Next, take up first weaver again and go around once, alternating with second weaver. Then take up second weaver again, then the first, and so on, weaving one at a time and alternating their positions. At end of each round, stop the weaver at the spoke just before you reach the other weaver, so that weavers will not cross.

DOUBLE UNDER-AND-OVER WEAVE (*below, Sketch 2, and page 52, Sketch 2*)

The double Under-and-Over Weave is the same as the single Under-and-Over except that two or four weavers, instead of one,

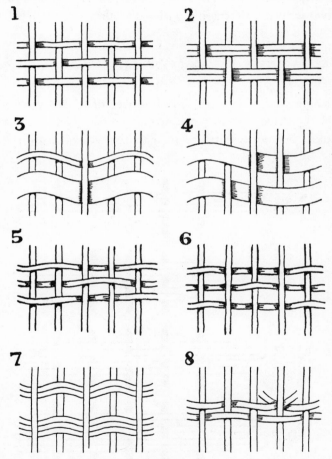

THE BASIC UNDER-AND-OVER WEAVES: (1) SINGLE UNDER-AND-OVER; (2) DOUBLE UNDER-AND-OVER; (3) SINGLE JAPANESE; (4) TWILL; (5) COLONIAL; (6) BELLEFONTE; (7) BAND; (8) PIECING UNDER-AND-OVER WEAVES

are carried along as a unit of weaving. Weave according to preceding directions. As in single Under-and-Over Weave, there
must be an odd number of spokes when the weaving material
consists of one pair or group of weavers, and an even number of
spokes when using two pairs of weavers, or two groups of more
than two weavers, alternating with each other.

SINGLE JAPANESE WEAVE (*page 51, Sketch 3, and below,
    Sketch 3*)

A single weaver is used. The number of spokes must not be
divisible by three; for instance, it may be twenty-five or twenty-
six spokes, but not twenty-seven. Pass the weaver in front of two

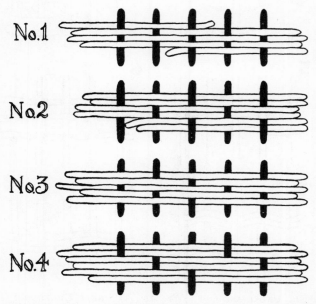

DETAILS OF STARTING AND FINISHING SOME OF THE BASIC WEAVES: (1)
SINGLE UNDER-AND-OVER; (2) DOUBLE UNDER-AND-OVER; (3) SINGLE

spokes and behind one. Continue thus, round after round. This weave is used also to start the Japanese base. It is shown (Sketch 3, page 51) with either a narrow or a wide weaver.

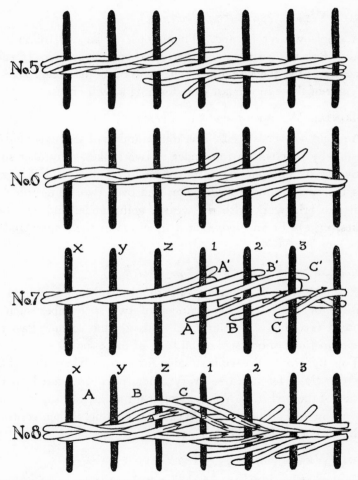

JAPANESE; (4) DOUBLE JAPANESE; (5) LAST ROW OF PAIRING; (6) LAST ROW OF TRIPLE; (7) LOCKING COIL; (8) FINISHING ARROW

Double Japanese Weave (*page 52, Sketch 4*)

Proceed exactly as in the single Japanese Weave, in front of two spokes and back of the next spoke, but use a pair of weavers instead of a single weaver.

Twill Weave (*page 51, Sketch 4*)

A single weaver is used. There must be an odd number of spokes. Pass the weaver under two spokes and over two. In each succeeding row, the weaving stitches will occur just one spoke to the right of those in the last row, forming a twill effect.

Colonial Weave (*page 51, Sketch 5*)

A single weaver is used. The total number of spokes should be divisible by four with a remainder of two spokes, a number such as twenty-six (24 plus 2) or thirty-four (32 plus 2), and so on. Pass the weaver under two spokes and over two. The effect is similar to brickwork with the weaver going under and over two spokes, instead of one spoke, at a time—as in the single Under-and-Over Weave.

Bellefonte Weave (*page 51, Sketch 6*)

A single weaver is used. The number of spokes should be divisible by four with a remainder of two, a number such as eighteen (16 plus 2) or thirty (28 plus 2), and so on. Pass the weaver in front of one spoke and back of three spokes.

This Bellefonte Weave is suitable for a space where the spokes are very close, for it leaves every other spoke uncovered on the outside of the basket. After weaving it for an inch or so, interrupt it by a row of Pairing, Triple Weave, or Coiling. Then continue with another section of Bellefonte Weave, if desired.

Band Weave (*page 51, Sketch 7*)

Groups of weavers are used. Sketch shows a group of two and a group of three weavers. The number of spokes may be odd or even. If an odd number, the spokes that were on the outside will be on the inside every other round, and the weave may continue as far as desired. If an even number, every other spoke will remain uncovered, and then the Band Weave, like the Bellefonte Weave, can be used for a limited space only.

PIECING WEAVERS IN UNDER-AND-OVER WEAVES (*page 51, Sketch* 8)

The old weaver terminates behind a spoke. Lay the new weaver beside it with its end projecting ½ inch at left of spoke, and proceed with new weaver.

PAIRING AND TWINING WEAVES

PAIRING WEAVE (*page 56, A*)

Two weavers are used. There may be either an odd or an even number of spokes. Pairing differs from the Under-and-Over Weave in that the weavers twist around each other as they go in and out of the spokes. The weaver at the left, or the rear weaver, comes out from under a spoke, passes over the next spoke, crosses over the other weave, while in the Under-and-Over Weave the weavers never cross. In the Pairing Weave begin with the left weaver, drawing it out from initial spoke to the outside. Do the same with the other weaver, bringing it out from the next spoke to the right. Pass each weaver in succession in front of the next spoke, across the other weaver, back of the next spoke, and out to the front. Finish each weaver behind the spoke from which it started (page 59, Sketch 5).

DOUBLE PAIRING WEAVE (*page 56, B*)

This weave is the same as the Pairing just described, except that two weavers are used together instead of one.

TRIPLE WEAVE (*below, Sketch C*)

This weave requires three weavers, and may be used over either an odd or an even number of spokes. The three weavers are started behind three consecutive spokes. Beginning at left pass each

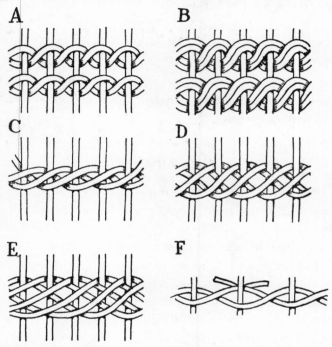

PAIRING WEAVES: (A) PAIRING; (B) DOUBLE PAIRING; (C) TRIPLE; (D) FOUR-ROD COIL; (E) FIVE-ROD COIL; (F) PIECING PAIRING WEAVES

weaver in succession in front of two spokes, crossing over the other two weavers, and passing back of next spoke. Triple Weave and Pairing Weave are similar except that three weavers are used in Triple Weave instead of the two used for Pairing, and each single weaver in Triple Weave passes over the other *two* weavers instead of over *one*, as in Pairing. (For last row of Triple Weave, see Sketch 6, page 53.)

Coil Weave (*page 56, Sketches D and E*)

A coil is a row of weaving resembling a rope or twist. It is simply a variation of Triple Weave with additional weavers. In a Three-rod Coil, use three weavers, and pass each weaver in front of two spokes and back of one. (This Three-rod Coil is also called Triple Weave.) In a Four-rod Coil, use four weavers and carry each in succession in front of three spokes and back of one. In a Five-rod Coil, pass each weaver in front of three spokes and back of two, or in front of four and back of one. In a Six-rod Coil, pass each weaver in front of four spokes and back of two. At the end of a coil the weavers are locked, as will be described.

Piecing Weavers in Pairing and Twining Weaves and Coils (*page 56, Sketch F*)

The old weaver terminates behind a spoke. Lay new weaver beside it with its end projecting ½ inch at left of spoke, and proceed with new weaver. Bring it out to front, crossing under the other weaver, then in front of next spoke, over the other weaver, and so on.

Locking a Coil

At the end of a coil or arrow, finish the several weavers so they will not show more than necessary. To do this, proceed as follows, consulting page 53, Sketch 7:

Back of three consecutive spokes—1, 2, and 3 (four spokes if Four-rod Coil is used)—are the three ends of the weavers at their start, *A*, *B*, and *C*, and the three ends at their finish, *A'*, *B'*, and *C'*.

Bring the first weaver *A'* from behind Spoke 1, under the other two weavers *B'* and *C'*. Lay it close beside, and parallel to, its own starting end *A* (arrow).

Bring the second weaver *B'* from behind Spoke 2, under weaver

C′, and also under *A* (in row below). Lay it close beside, and parallel to, its own starting end *B* (arrow).

Bring the third weaver *C′*, from behind Spoke 3, under weavers *A* and *B* (in row below) and lay it close beside, and parallel to, its own starting end *C* (arrow).

As each weaver thus returns to its own starting end after its last stitch, the entire row of coiling is made complete with no break in its ropelike effect.

Arrow Weave (*page 53, Sketch 8, and page 59*).

In this type of weave, the stitches converge at each spoke, forming lines similar to arrows. The Arrow Weave may be made by weaving a row of Triple with a second row having the weavers reversed; or by weaving a row of any coil with a second row having its weavers reversed. Several steps are necessary to prepare weavers for the second row, or the row with the weavers moving in reverse directions. When weaving Arrow Weave, cut weavers twice as long as the distance around the basket, for there are two complete rows; also add a few inches to allow for the beginning and the end.

Preparatory Steps for Second Row of Arrow Weave (*page 59*)

The starting spoke is labeled Spoke 1; the other spokes are labeled from left to right, 2, 3, 4, 5, and 6. The last spoke before reaching Spoke 1 is labeled Z.

Step 1. Finish first weaver *A* back of spoke where it started (see *A′* behind Spoke 1, top sketch); carry it out to front over previous row where it stands ready for weaving (see *A′*, dotted lines, and arrow moving downward, center sketch).

Step 2. Finish second weaver *B* back of spoke where it started (see *B′* behind Spoke 2, top sketch); carry it out to front over previous row and ready for weaving (see *B'*; also arrow moving downward, and dotted lines, center sketch).

Step 3. Finish third weaver *C* back of spoke where it started (see *C'* behind Spoke 3, top sketch); carry it out to front over

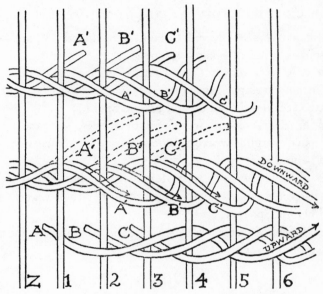

PREPARATORY STEPS OF SECOND ROW, ARROW WEAVE

previous row and ready for weaving (see *C'*, dotted lines, and arrow moving downward, center sketch).

Step 4. If the coil is a Four-rod Coil, finish fourth weaver back of spoke where it started; carry it out to front over previous row and ready for weaving.

Weavers are now out in front ready for second or reverse round (see arrows). For this round, carry weaver *A'* over Spokes 2 and 3, *under* the other two weavers *B'* and *C'* (instead of over them as in regular first round), and back of Spoke 4 (top sketch). Carry weaver *B'* over Spokes 3 and 4, *under* the other two weavers *C'* and *A'*, and behind Spoke 5 (center sketch). Carry weaver *C'* over Spokes 4 and 5, *under* the other two weavers *A'* and *B'*, and behind Spoke 6 (center sketch). Continue thus with each weaver in succession.

FINISH OF THE ARROW WEAVE (*follow Sketch* 8, *page* 53)

Finish weavers *A*, *B*, and *C* back of Spokes *X*, *Y*, and *Z* (the three spokes at left of Spokes 1, 2, and 3).

Step 1. Carry weaver *C*, at right, over Spokes 1 and 2, close beside its converging weaver in row below (see arrows), under the other two weavers *B* and *C*, and behind Spoke 3.

Step 2. Carry second weaver *B* over Spokes Z and 1, close beside its converging weaver, under the other two weavers *A* and *C*, and behind next Spoke 2.

Step 3. Carry weaver *A*, at left, over Spokes *Y* and Z, close beside its converging weaver, under the other two weavers *B* and *C*, and behind Spoke 1.

Each finishing weaver is thus tucked in to complete the round of converging arrows.

PRACTICE WORK

When mastered, the preceding weaves become the working key to all the weaving projects in this book. Practice work may be carried on by the use of cord, rope, paper, rags, and other materials to avoid unnecessary waste of reed or raffia. However, you may use reed and unwind it for use again. Resoak it each time before using.

CHAPTER 9

BORDERS

A RHYTHMIC WOVEN border with all reeds smoothly turned and all ends firmly fastened completes a basket. To make this border, see that the spokes are well soaked and flexible. If they do not bend easily, use pincers at bending points to secure turnings without breaking.

BORDER 1 (*Sketch* 1). (See page 62 for illustrations of Borders 1–5.)

Sharpen points of spokes and trim all to the same length. Soak until flexible. Bend each spoke in succession in a loop extending 1 to 2 inches above top row of weaving. Tuck each end down into the weaving beside the next spoke at right. When all ends are tucked in, turn basket upside down and press against table to make the border loops even.

BORDER 2 (*Sketch* 2)

Sharpen points of spokes and trim them all to the same length. Soak well. Bend each spoke in succession in a loop and tuck its end down beside the third spoke at right, as in Sketch 2.

BORDER 3 (*Sketch* 3)

Follow directions for Border 2, but tuck each spoke down beside fourth instead of third spoke.

BORDER 4 (*Sketch* 4)

1st row. Carry each spoke back of the spoke at its right; repeat all around basket. When you come to last spoke, carry it behind loop of first spoke already turned down.

2nd row. Carry each spoke (now on the outside) to inside of basket and in front of next spoke at its right; repeat all around basket. When you come to last spoke, carry it in front of loop of first spoke.

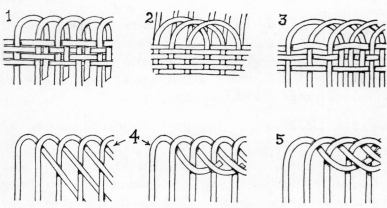

FIVE SIMPLE BASKET BORDERS

BORDER 5 (*Sketch 5*)

1st row. Follow directions for first row in Border 4.

2nd row. Carry each spoke (now on outside of basket) in front of second and third spokes at its right, and to inside of basket.

3rd row. The ends of the spokes (now on inside of basket) may be further secured by bending each end down over the end at its right. This edge may be used as an inside finish to secure the ends of any border.

ROLLED OR COMMERCIAL BORDER (*pages 63 and 64*)

Step 1. Carry a spoke, such as Spoke 1, back of next spoke at right, and out. Repeat for Spoke 2. Both spokes now project toward the front.

Step 2. Carry Spoke 1 in front of vertical Spoke 3, across projecting Spoke 2, and behind vertical Spoke 4, and then out to the front. Hold down Spokes 1 and 2 while bending down Spoke 3

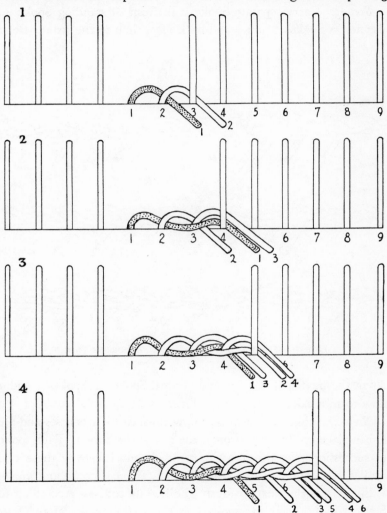

DETAIL OF ROLLED OR COMMERCIAL BORDER (see also next page)

back of vertical Spoke 4 (diagram, Step 2). Spokes 2, 1, and 3 are now projected toward the front. Projecting Spoke 2, at left, is separate from 1 and 3.

Step 3. Carry separate Spoke 2 in front of standing Spoke 4; also across Spokes 1 and 3 and back of 5, then to the front. Bend

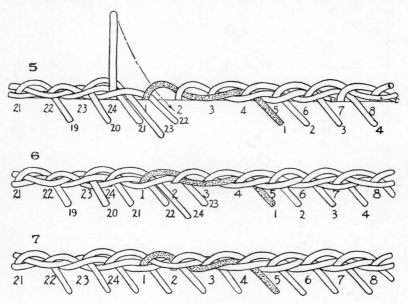

DETAIL OF ROLLED OR COMMERCIAL BORDER (*cont.*)

down the next spoke (4) behind vertical Spoke 5. Spokes 1 and 3 now form a pair, while 2 and 4 form another pair.

Step 4. Spokes 1 and 2 have now finished their courses and are left in place until trimmed off at the end of the border. Each spoke in succession goes through the turns already taken by these two spokes, and shown by the shaded spoke (1) on page 63 and *above*.

Spoke 3 is the next to finish. Follow its course. According to Step 3 of the diagram, Spoke 3 is the second spoke of the four 1, 3, 2, and 4) that are now bent out toward the front. Carry this second projecting spoke (3) in front of first standing spoke (5), across the other pair (2 and 4), back of next standing spoke (6), and out to the front. The result of this procedure will be the arrangement shown in the diagram, Step 4.

Carry the first standing spoke (5) back of the next standing spoke (6), and out parallel to the spoke (3) which has just been brought to its last position. Carry Spoke 4 (the one at the right in the group of four projecting spokes—1, 3, 2, 4—seen in the diagram, Step 3) in front of vertical Spoke 6, back of 7, and out to the front. Carry vertical Spoke 6 back of 7, and down parallel to 4. There are now, as in Step 3, two pairs of spokes bent downward. This time the pairs are 3 and 5, 4 and 6. When a spoke is left single in front, after its parallel spoke has been carried ahead, it is completed. Observe single Spoke 1 and single Spoke 2 in Step 4.

From now on carry the second spoke (such as 5), of the four bent down in groups of two (3 and 5, 4 and 6) in front of the first standing spoke (7), across the other pair, back of the next standing spoke (8), and out parallel to the spoke just brought down. There are now two new pairs in front. Repeat the procedure, just outlined in this paragraph, to the end of the border.

Step 5. At the end of this border, be certain that the progress of each spoke is completed. In Step 5, the final upright spoke (24) is brought down under Spoke 1 and parallel to 22 (see diagram). Spoke 23 now becomes the second spoke of the two pairs (21 and 23, 22 and 24). These numbers refer to any last spokes.

Step 6. Observe in the diagram that Spoke 23 is brought in front of 1, across the other pair of spokes (22 and 24), back of Spoke 2, and out to the front.

Step 7. Bring Spoke 24 in front of 2, across the projecting Spoke 23, back of Spoke 3, and out to the front, thus completing the border, as shown in the diagram, Step 7.

CHAPTER 10

TRAY WEAVING

TRAYS ARE always useful, and no home is complete without them. The making of a tray is used as the first basketry project because the tray is such a practical item and is easier to make than the basket forms. Since the tray base is already prepared, all you need do is to select the shape and size, insert the spokes of the basket in its bored holes, take a few rows of stitches for the sides, and finish off the spokes in an attractive border for the top.

Some of the many tray forms available at basket supply houses are shown on page 67 and page 68. You may make any of these yourself with a jig saw. For a first basket let us make a bread tray on a small, simple, oval base.

SMALL BREAD TRAY (page 69)

MATERIALS

Oval base of 3-ply wood $7\frac{1}{2}$ inches wide and $14\frac{1}{2}$ inches long. Bore thirty-eight holes in base for No. 3 reed, $\frac{1}{4}$ inch from edge and $\frac{3}{4}$ to 1 inch apart.

DIMENSIONS

Spokes—No. 3 reed. Cut thirty-eight uprights, 12 inches long.
Weavers—No. 2 reed. Have ready six to twelve lengths.
Handle—No. 2 reed, two pieces for winding. No. 6 reed, one piece for body.

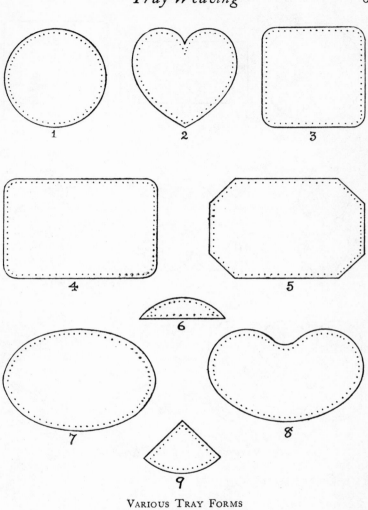

VARIOUS TRAY FORMS
(See also next page.)

EQUIPMENT

Use regular tools as listed in Chapter 5.

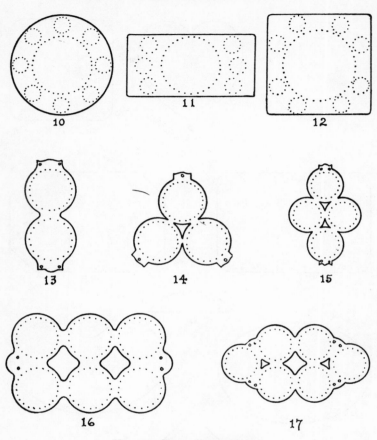

VARIOUS TRAY FORMS (*cont.*)

TIME CONSUMED

Learning time, about thirty minutes.

Time for completing project, about two hours.

STARTING TRAY

In cutting the reed for spokes, make pointed ends. Straighten these uprights and soak 3 inches of their lower ends by placing in a jar of tepid water for fifteen minutes. When ends are pliable and will bend without breaking, wipe off the moisture with a soft cloth. Then insert into holes of tray base, with $2\frac{1}{2}$ inches of ends extending below base. Turn basket upside down (*below, A*). If necessary, squeeze spokes with pincers at bending points to

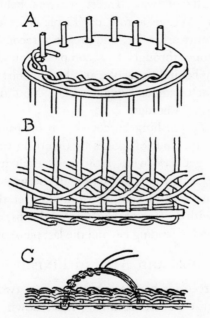

DETAILS IN THE WEAVING OF A SMALL BREAD TRAY

insure complete bending over close to base. Bend these ends in and toward the left, putting each end in front of first spoke at left and back of second spoke. Continue thus until all ends are bound and woven firmly underneath the tray. Bend last end in front of the first spoke and behind the second.

Press the twisted ends firmly down against the base and draw spokes tightly around the basket to tie them smoothly to the base. Now turn basket right side up and weave the sides. Straighten each spoke and bend, one at a time, slightly outwards before weaving.

WEAVING SIDES OF TRAY AND BORDER

With three pieces of No. 2 reed, start weaving at the center of the longer side of oval. Insert weavers behind three consecutive spokes. Weave a row of Triple Weave (page 69, *B*). Bend uprights outward a bit, and weave a second row of Triple Weave. Continue through five complete rounds. Bring each weaver to a stop behind the spoke at which it started, and nip each end so that $\frac{1}{2}$ inch extends beyond spoke. You are now ready to roll the spokes into a border.

Use the simple finishing border shown on page 62, Sketch 4. First, soak well the ends of spokes by inverting tray over a tub of water; do not get base wet. Now bend each upright over and back of the one at its right, and down all the way around. Repeat for a second and a third complete round. Let the tray dry and trim off ends with a slanting cut against the basket, leaving $\frac{1}{4}$ to $\frac{1}{2}$ inch of each end extending beyond the last piece of reed it touches.

MAKING HANDLE AND ADDING FINISH

The No. 6 reed for handle is now cut into two pieces 8 inches long, and their ends are pointed. Push down into pockets of weaving at the ends, making a semicircle of the handle with its ends about 3 inches apart (page 69, *C*). Trim off until of the desired height. Double over a piece of No. 2 reed and loop this around a spoke below the base and under one end of handle. Bring ends up through the weaving and wrap around the handle-rod, making wrappings close together or separating at even distances. Carry each in and out so that it will not show but will be firmly fastened.

The tray may be waxed, painted, or stained. It is effective when covered with black filler, allowed to dry, sandpapered, then covered with a coat of black enamel. A floral motif of bright color may be painted or stenciled in the center.

LARGE OVAL TRAY

The only difference between the large tray and the small one just described is in the size of the base, the number of spokes, and the number of weaving rows.

MATERIALS

Base—Oval shape of 3-ply wood like Sketch 7 (page 67), $10\frac{1}{2}$ inches wide and 20 inches long. Bore base with forty-eight holes for No. 4 reed $\frac{1}{4}$ inch from outer edge and $\frac{3}{4}$ to 1 inch apart.

Spokes—Forty-eight spokes No. 4 reed, 14 inches long.

Weavers—No. 3 reed, six to twelve pieces.

Handles—Two pieces No. 2 for winding. One piece No. 6 for foundation body.

TIME REQUIRED

About two and one-half hours.

MAKING TRAY

Cut out and straighten reeds, then insert spokes in base, turning ends under and weaving sides as you did in making smaller tray (page 69). Make six rows of Triple Weave around sides. Make a similar border. Set handles in the same way, one at each end. Before finishing, carefully trim off ends and singe any hairy extensions, being watchful not to burn basket.

OBLONG OR SQUARE TRAYS

Oblong or square trays are handled like oval trays. Use care at the corners, keeping them pulled out in as square a form as possible. For an oblong tray, use a base of the shape shown in Sketch 4, page 67. This base is 12 inches wide and $18\frac{1}{2}$ inches long. Cut fifty-six spokes of No. 4 reed, 14 inches long. Bore holes ¼ inch from edges. Set one spoke at each corner; ten spokes between corners of tray ends; sixteen spokes between corners on long sides. Use No. 3 weavers; make six rows of weaving for sides. Finish border as described for oval trays. Trim and singe entire tray. For finishing, see Chapter 3.

MAKING TRAY BASES

Various base shapes may be found in basket catalogues or in museums. You may purchase these shapes at regular basketry

THREE USEFUL BASKETS
A jardiniere basket with flowers; a small round cake or bread basket, and a two-handled tray woven over a wooden base.

supply houses, or make them at home, or have them made by a carpenter.

The wood used in making bases should be 3-ply, of maple, bass, or birch, well seasoned, light, and free from knots, cracks, and twists. The following implements are needed to make them: Saw, coping saw, brace and bit, or drill, jack and block planes, sandpaper, try square and compass, a foot rule, and a measuring line.

OTHER BASKET FORMS

Many forms may be used in the creating of baskets. These may be drawn on paper, or wooden models of them may be made around which to build part of the basket. You may also use cooking kettles, vases, or blocks of wood for guiding the sides in effective curves. Some of the most frequently used forms are concave, convex, round, oval, bowl-shape, cone, pyramid, cylinder, and plate. Objects copied are jugs, crocks, wheels, animals, squares, rectangles, birds, fish, and boats.

Baskets also take the place of other articles made of wood or metal. The commercial forms that may serve as guides are fruit and flower baskets, mirrors, clothes hampers, coaster bases, foot rests, umbrella stands, desk trays, and lamp forms for table, shelf, wall, or floor. These special patterns meet the special needs of the advanced weaver.

CHAPTER 11

JARDINIERE BASKET

JARDINIERE BASKETS may be made in various sizes and in different shapes—round, square, bowl-shaped, oval, and six-sided. A jardiniere makes not only a practical but also an artistic basket to cover the container of a house plant or fern.

MATERIALS

Base—Wooden base of 3-ply wood, 8 inches in diameter. Bore nineteen holes for No. 4 reed, ¾ inch from outer edge.

Spokes—Cut nineteen spokes of No. 4 reed, 22 inches long. Cut nineteen seconds, or bi-spokes, of No. 4 reed, 17 inches long.

Weavers—About one-half pound No. 3 reed.

STEPS IN WEAVING

Base—Soak the reed in warm water. Insert the spokes in holes of base with ends extending 2½ inches below it. Fasten down spoke-ends (page 69, Sketch *A*).

Sides—Before weaving the sides, draw all spokes up tightly under base and press down against table to make a smooth edge. Rest basket on table while weaving sides.

Straighten the uprights and bend them out gradually while weaving up the sides. Begin by using No. 3 reed. Start next to base with either two rounds of Triple Weave or a Coil, as described in Chapter 8. Press these rows down firmly, and insert the seconds, or bi-spokes, on left side of each of nineteen uprights.

Now start regular Triple Weave again over the pairs of spokes. Continue up the sides, bending spokes in shape shown, until the

74

basket is 8 inches high. As the distance between the spokes widens, separate spokes into single spokes and continue Triple Weave until the greatest width of basket at shoulders measures 15 inches in diameter. At this point bend spokes inward, until diameter across top opening measures 12 inches.

BORDER

Cut out all bi-spokes flush with last row of weaving, and use only regular spokes for border.

Turn uprights from left to right as follows: Bend Spoke 1 over 2, and to inside of basket behind 3. Bend Spoke 2 over 3, and to inside of basket behind 4.

Continue thus with each spoke until you have worked all around the basket. Bend last spoke over loop made by Spoke 1 and behind 2. Make a second round like this first round. This second round makes an inner roll beneath the border, and holds all spokes firmly (Chapter 9, page 62).

After finishing border, turn basket upside down on table, and press down to be sure that top of border lies level all around.

STAINING

This jardiniere basket may be stained with seal brown or dark green dye, or a mixture of both. Mix, stir, and dip three times, as in staining wastebaskets. In mixing the seal brown and green, use two packages of brown and one of green. This quantity should dye eighteen jardiniere baskets.

When the basket is dry, shellac it inside and out.

CHAPTER 12

WASTE OR SCRAP BASKETS

SINCE SCRAP baskets are used as receptacles for discarded materials of home, office, and shop, their size, color, shape, and weight should be determined by the purpose they are to serve. These baskets are shaped into round, oval, oblong, square, and bowl forms.

ROUND SCRAP BASKET, MODEL 1

MATERIALS

Base—One 10-inch base of 3-ply wood with twenty-one holes bored for No. 5 reed.

Spokes—Cut twenty-one spokes of No. 5 reed 29 inches long. Cut twenty-one bi-spokes 27 inches long.

Weavers—About one-fourth pound No. 4; about one-half pound ¾-inch flat reed for weavers.

WEAVING

Base—Straighten the uprights and soak 3 inches of one end. Straighten the bi-spokes and soak well. When uprights are sufficiently flexible to bend without breaking, put them through the holes in the base and bind into place by the Under-and-Over method (illustrated on page 69, Chapter 10).

Sides—Weave two rows of Triple Weave, using No. 4 weavers. Insert the bi-spokes on the left side of the uprights. Weave thirteen additional rows of Triple Weave, using each pair of uprights to weave around as if there were only one. Then weave three rows of flat reed in Under-and-Over Weave. Then fifteen rows of No. 4 reed in Triple Weave.

Border—Finish the basket by making the border as follows:

1st row—Soak and pinch spokes close to the last weaver. Bring each upright in succession in front of next three spokes at right and to the inside.

2nd row—Weave each spoke in succession over the next two spokes and bend it down on the inside.

Place the basket on the table and test for trueness of circle. If the weaving is uneven, the basket must be forced into shape to true up the opening. Place a flat board over the top with weights on it, and allow basket to dry in this position. When thoroughly dry, singe, trim, stain, and shellac. Then dry, wrap, and store for future use.

SCRAP BASKET, MODEL 2

For Model 2, use the same kind of base, same number of holes, same length of uprights, and same kind of round and flat reed as in Model 1. But change the weaving of the sides as follows: From the base, weave fifteen rows of No. 4 round reed in Triple Weave, twelve rows of flat reed in single Under-and-Over Weave, and thirteen rows of No. 4 round reed in Triple Weave. Make the border the same as in Model 1, and similarly test, dry, trim, singe, and stain with commercial dye, using three dippings and one coat of shellac.

SCRAP BASKET, MODEL 3 *(page 78)*

For Model 3, use the same base measurements, same number and length of uprights, and same size of weavers, both round and flat, as for Models 1 and 2. In weaving the sides of the basket use the following:

Thirteen rows of No. 4 reed in Triple Weave.

Sixteen rows of flat reed in Under-and-Over Weave, using pairs of weavers.

Eleven rows of No. 4 reed in Triple Weave.

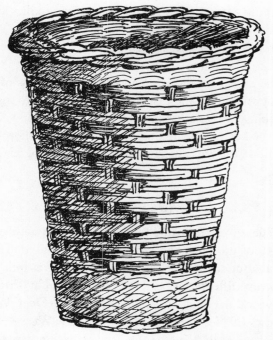

SCRAP BASKET, MODEL 3. NOTE PATTERN OF WEAVING AND
GRADUAL WIDENING OF DISTANCES BETWEEN SPOKES

Finish the border of the basket by plaiting the top as in Model 1. Test, dry, trim, singe, and stain. Dry and shellac.

BOUDOIR BASKET

MATERIALS

Base—One 8-inch base of 3-ply wood with nineteen holes

bored for No. 5 reed. The boudoir basket may also be made on an oval base.

Spokes—Use No. 5 reed for uprights. Cut nineteen spokes, 28 inches long. Cut nineteen seconds, 26 inches long.

Weavers—Use No. 4 reed for one set of weavers. Use flat ¾-inch reed for second set of weavers.

WEAVING

Base—Straighten uprights and soak 3 inches of the ends. Thread the spokes through holes of base, and bind them down to base by the Under-and-Over method (page 69).

Sides—Weave two rows No. 4 reed in Triple Weave. Insert seconds on the left side of the uprights. Weave fourteen rows Triple Weave, using No. 4 reed. Weave fourteen rows flat reed, using the Under-and-Over Weave. Weave fifteen rows Triple Weave, using No. 4 reed.

The basket should measure 10½ inches in diameter at the top without the border. Before weaving border, shape top into a circle with a diameter of 10½ inches. The height should be 12 inches and should measure the same on all four sides.

Border—Same as for Model 1. True up and allow to dry. When thoroughly dry, trim and singe. To color or stain use packaged dye, and dip three times. After basket is dry, shellac inside and out.

BORDER VARIATIONS

1*st round.* Use ends of uprights and bi-spokes in pairs after they have been thoroughly soaked. Weave from left to right, carrying the first pair back of the second pair and down; carry second pair back of third pair and down, and so on, until first round of border is complete. The ends should be on outside of basket.

2nd round. Bring first pair over second and third pairs, back of fourth pair, and then in. Bring second pair over both third and fourth pairs, back of fifth pair, and in. Continue around basket until border is complete. The ends should be on inside of basket. To bring ends outside of basket, slip first pair of spokes over second pair, under third pair, and out; slip second pair over third pair, under fourth pair, and out. Repeat until every pair of spokes has been brought to outside of basket around entire border. Then lock ends. True up while wet, allow to dry, trim, singe, and stain.

RING HANDLES

Select one piece of No. 5 reed that has been thoroughly soaked. Make it into a ring 2½ inches in diameter by twisting the reed around itself as many times as is necessary to use two-thirds of its entire length. Use the remainder of the weaver for winding

YOUNG WOMEN WEAVING BASKETS IN AN OUTDOOR CLASS

around and binding the ring in an artistic coil. Make a second ring exactly like the first and bind these rings on two opposite sides of basket, just below the braid border, with a piece of No. 3 reed made double and thoroughly soaked. The ring handles will hang loosely, like earrings, from just under the basket border.

CHAPTER 13

FLOWER BASKETS

VASE BASKET MADE OVER TUMBLER (*page* 83)

MATERIALS

Spokes—Sixteen spokes of No. 3 reed 30 inches long, and two spokes 16 inches long.

Weavers—No. 1 reed.

Handles—Two pieces No. 5 reed 25 to 30 inches long. Glass jar or tumbler with 2-inch base.

STEPS IN WEAVING

Base—The base is made a little larger than the base of the glass, and is turned up around the glass in such a way as to hold it firmly. Make the Indian Basket Base (Chapter 6, pages 40 and 41). Use the Under-and-Over Weave. Carry the spokes in pairs. When base measures $\frac{1}{2}$ inch less than its final diameter, add three rows of Triple Weave. This strengthens the edge. If this does not bring the base out just beyond the outside of glass, add a fourth row.

Sides—Soak spokes of base, bend up around tumbler, and weave four rows, about $\frac{1}{2}$ inch, of Pairing Weave (page 83, *A*). Draw rows taut. Add two more weavers and put in one round, about $\frac{1}{4}$ inch, of a Four-rod Coil (*B*). Add eight rows of Pairing, about 1 inch (*C*). Then add a Three-rod Arrow, about $\frac{3}{8}$ inch (*D*). At this point leave pairs of spokes uncovered for a space of 2 inches (*E*). Bring them together again with another Three-rod Arrow

(*F*). Add eight rows of Pairing (*G*). Spread out as necessary to surround glass container, and make shape graceful. The last row should rise just above the top of the tumbler.

Border—(*H*). Soak spokes well. Weave them in pairs as follows:

1*st row*. Carry first pair back of second pair to outside; carry second pair back of third pair to outside, and so on. Continue all around border.

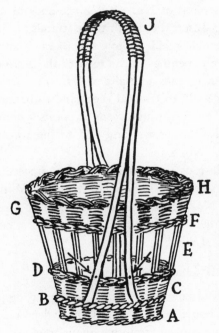

VASE BASKET MADE OVER TUMBLER

2*nd row*. Weave first pair over second pair, and to inside and back of third pair; weave second pair over third pair, and to inside and back of fourth pair, and so on. Continue thus all around border.

3rd row. Carry first pair over second pair and down; carry second pair over third pair and down; and continue all around basket until border is complete and locked at point of starting. To lock border, carry last pair over the loop of first pair and down.

Singe basket, trim, and true up its shape; then dry.

Handles—(*J*). Measure and point up basket, marking centers of opposite sides. The handle-rods are inserted through Three-rod Arrow (*D*), and the Four-rod Coil (*B*). Use two strands of No. 5 reed, or three strands of No. 4. Whittle ends to tapering points; soak reeds well. Insert the two or three strands to make a fan-shape about $1\frac{1}{4}$ to $1\frac{1}{2}$ inches wide on one side of vase, passing the strands carefully through openings in the rows of the Arrow and the Coil. Carry the tapering ends to right or left and into the horizontal weaving of Coil (*B*), to conceal them and to make handle secure. A hole may be bored through reeds at points where they cross the Three-rod Coil (see arrows) and tied to the weaving with well-soaked No. 0 or No. 1 reed.

Carry handle-rods up over basket in a graceful curve. Insert ends on second side, opposite those of first side. Wind top of handle with No. 0 or No. 1 reed soaked until pliable. Use the figure-of-eight winding method (shown at *J*). Fasten last end of reed back under last inch of winding.

STAINING AND DECORATING

Take out glass container. Stain basket by dipping into commercial dye. Choose seal brown, maroon, deep red, green, or any dark color. One package will dye about four articles of this size, with three dippings allowed for each. Follow directions, adding 1 gallon of boiling water to dissolved dye. Stir well. Dip basket three times, drying well after each dipping. When thoroughly dry, shellac basket both inside and out. Any shaping must be done after the last dipping, and before the shellac finish is added. Replace glass container.

Such basket vases may also be given a coat of oil paint in a cheery color, but care must be taken to use a brush that will carry the paint well down into the crevices of the basket stitches.

BUD VASE (*page* 86)

MATERIALS

One test tube about 7 inches long and 1 inch in diameter. Eight pieces No. 3 reed, 17 inches long, for uprights. Cut ends of these diagonally.

Three pieces No. 2 reed for weavers.

One wide rubber band or heavy cord.

TOOLS

Scissors, nippers, knife, tape measure.

WEAVING THE VASE

Main Part of Base—When weaving main part of vase, use spokes dry; but when weaving base, soak lower ends; and when weaving border, soak upper ends.

Put the eight uprights in place around the test tube with ends extending $2\frac{1}{4}$ inches below and $2\frac{1}{2}$ inches above the top of the tube. Hold these uprights tightly in position with an elastic band or string (page 86, *A*). Separate spokes an equal distance apart. Turn vase upside down. Now take a No. 2 weaver, well soaked, and double it around one of the uprights $1\frac{1}{4}$ inches below top of test tube (as at *a* and *b*). With top of tube toward weaver, weave from left to right, using Pairing Weave.

Sides and Top Border—Weave eight to ten rounds of Pairing Weave, working *away* from rubber band toward top. Last row should be even with top of tube, with $2\frac{1}{2}$ inches of spokes extending beyond it.

It is a good plan at this point to make the top border, in order to get extending spokes out of the way. Soak upper ends of spokes.

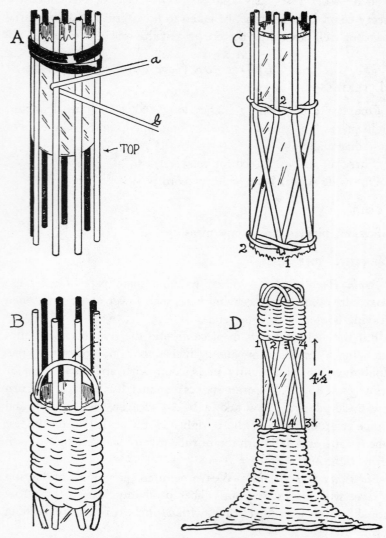

STEPS IN WEAVING A BASKET BUD VASE OVER A TEST TUBE

Bend each spoke down in a loop, over two spokes at its left, and in beside third spoke (see arrows at *B*). Make loops $\frac{1}{2}$ inch high. Continue all around top. Even up all loops by inverting vase and pressing top against table.

Weaving Sides and Base—Start lower section of weaving (page 86, *C*, 1 and 2) $4\frac{1}{2}$ inches below upper section. Arrange spokes in layers, laying spokes of each pair across each other, as shown by cross made by Spokes 1 and 2. To weave this section (see *D*), turn basket with top toward you. Use a well-soaked strand of No. 2, bent double. Start Pairing. Weave around the spokes, first over crossed Spoke 1, then over 2, and so on. Continue thus all around vase, for six rows.

To widen base into flare shown, add spokes at this point. Cut eight bi-spokes 6 inches long, and insert one beside each regular spoke. Weave two rows around these as double spokes, then separate all spokes and weave with Pairing Weave around the sixteen single ones. Shove spokes down on a table while working to make them flare outward, and continue making shape (*D*) until there are about twenty rows of weaving in the base section and until the vase measures 3 to 4 inches in diameter.

Base Border—Use same border as that given for top, or choose one of the borders given in Chapter 9 (illustrated on page 62).

STAINING AND FINISHING

Stain with a light wood-stain, or paint with a pastel blue, lavender, rose, or green oil paint. Test tube should fit snugly, but may be removed for the finishing. You may also dye the reed before starting the basket. After basket is thoroughly dry, it may be shellacked.

BASKET HOLDER FOR POTTED PLANTS (*page* 88)

Flower baskets add beauty to the bouquets they hold, and spring is a good time to prepare for garden blossoms. A basket made for an azalea or a lily will be found useful all the year long. In the summer it may hold tumblers filled with cut flowers, and in the winter window plants may be placed in it. The basket is simply made, and several baskets may be woven from the list of supplies given here.

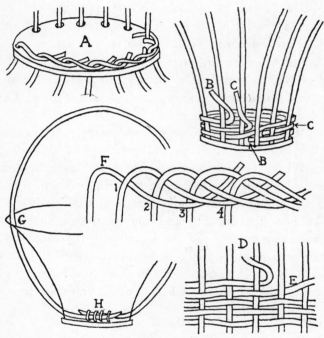

<small>STEPS IN WEAVING A BASKET HOLDER FOR POTTED PLANTS</small>

MATERIALS

Round basket base 5 inches in diameter, bored for No. 4 reed. Or a base can be made from 3-ply wood, 5 inches in diameter, with holes bored $\frac{1}{4}$ inch from edge and $\frac{3}{4}$ inch apart. Make an even number of holes.

Sixteen ounces No. 4 reed.

Sixteen ounces No. 3 reed.

Weaving the Basket

Base and Sides—Use No. 4 reed for spokes, as many spokes as there are holes in your base, and cut these 16 inches long. Soak spokes one hour and dry in a towel, so as not to wet the base. Insert spokes in holes, leaving 3 inches below base. Turn basket over and lap each end over the end at its right, and tuck in (page 88, *A*).

Take strand of No. 3 reed, well soaked. Use Under-and-Over Weave with two weavers for an even number of spokes. Insert strand *B* (as at arrow, page 88); pass in and out of spokes all around basket, and back to beginning. Hold here; start strand *C* at next spoke to right, inserted behind spoke that *B* went over. Weave *C* all around and back to spoke at left of waiting spoke, *B*. Now hold *C*, while *B* goes around. Stop at each spoke at left of other strand while this proceeds; *D* stops as *E* continues, and so on (follow sketches, page 88, *C*).

Weave upward thus until basket is 6 or more inches high, flaring gently outward. To add a new strand, simply lap the new end alongside the old, behind a spoke.

Border—Soak well the tops of spokes. Pass each spoke (begin at *F*) under spoke at its right; pass Spoke 1 over Spokes 2 and 3, and under 4. Repeat on all spokes; pull up tightly; tuck in last end.

Handle (E)—Take three strands No. 4, or one strand No. 7 or No. 8 reed, 42 inches long. Whittle ends and insert one end of the group through the weaving just above the board. Interweave three ends into basket for 2 inches. Push other ends up through border (*G*), twist together, carry around to other side, down through border, then to bottom of basket. Interlace ends (see *H*). It is also possible to use a single, larger strand thus, whittling ends flat. Shellac when thoroughly dry.

CHAPTER 14

HANGING BASKETS

SMALL HANGING BASKET (page 91)

MATERIALS

Six center spokes No. 4 reed, 5 inches long.
One piece No. 2 reed (weaver for base).
No. 3 weaver for sides.
Twelve uprights of No. 4 reed, 25 inches long.
Twelve spokes of No. 4 reed, 20 inches long.
Three pieces of No. 3 reed for 24-inch handle.
One piece No. 3 reed for handle ring.

STEPS IN WEAVING

Cup-shaped Base—Soak six center spokes of No. 4 reed, and one piece No. 2 reed. Pierce holes in three spokes and run other spokes through the first three to form button for the base. Take No. 2 reed and weave around these crossed spokes, using the Pairing Weave. Cup-shape the base and bring to a rounded point. Insert the twelve uprights of No. 4 reed into the sides about $1\frac{1}{2}$ inches from the center. With No. 3 reed, weave the sides in Pairing Weave. Continue until the sides measure 5 inches from the bottom point.

Now add twelve new spokes, 20 inches long, one beside each old spoke. This gives twenty-four spokes to weave over. Weave 4 inches more, using Triple Weave. While weaving up the sides, shape basket gradually from the bottom so that it will measure

2 inches in diameter at the base, 8½ inches at its greatest diameter, and 7½ inches across the top. The depth of the basket should be about 7 inches. The length of the finished handle should be about 24 inches.

Upper Part and Border—To make the band at top of basket, insert extra spokes, one beside each of the twelve pairs of spokes, which gives a total of thirty-six spokes. At two opposite points of basket, leave one spoke alone. Make one more round of Triple Weave over the thirty-four spokes (seventeen pairs) and the two single spokes opposite each other; then cut off the two singles, leaving thirty-four spokes for Bellefonte Weave, which consists in passing a single weaver in front of one spoke and back of three spokes (see Chapter 8 for weave description, and page 51, Sketch 6). This procedure results in an attractive band with pairs of spokes showing. Weave the band 1 inch high. Finish with one round of Triple Weave.

HANGING BASKET

For border, pass each pair of spokes over the pair at its right and to inside of basket. Make one complete round. Make a second round like the first on the inside edge.

Handle—For the handle, first make a twisted ring of No. 3

reed 1½ inches in diameter. Take three pieces of No. 3 reed, and double each through the ring. Then twist the doubled strands of reed around each other until all three parts of the handle are made into firmly twisted ropes. Lock or weave the three ends into the sides of the basket through and under the border. The handles may also be fastened to the basket by means of three twisted rings, placed equidistant on the border of the basket.

FINISHING BASKET

After the basket has been woven and the handle placed, true it up, singe, stain, and decorate. If the basket is to be used for flowers or plants, you will need a watertight tin or galvanized container for the inside. (See page 94 for shapes of watertight containers.)

BOWL-SHAPED HANGING BASKET
(*page* 93, *Sketch* 4)

MATERIALS

No. 3 reed for uprights.
No. 2 reed for weavers.
No. 1 reed to start center.
Flat winding reed, approximately ⅛ inch in width.

This basket is suggested by the outline given on page 93, Sketch 4. It can be made entirely of round reed, or flat reed may be used in the upper part to add variety of texture. The basket measurements are: 10 inches from lowest point to the border at the rim; diameter at widest point, 9½ inches; and diameter at the top border, 8½ inches.

STEPS IN WEAVING

Base—Cut eight spokes of No. 3 reed 35 inches long. Straighten and point these at the ends. Soak one piece of No. 1 reed; also

No. 2 and some flat winding reed. With an awl, pierce four spokes
at their centers, making a slit 1 inch long. From this point follow
directions for Japanese Base (Chapter 6, and illustration on

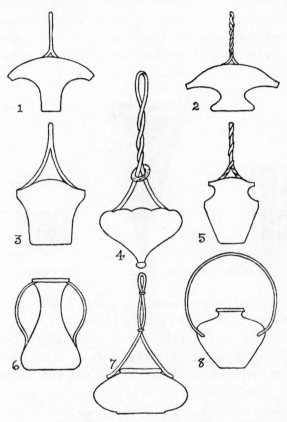

SUGGESTED DESIGNS FOR HANGING BASKETS

page 37). Use No. 1 reed for starting, and transfer to No. 2 later,
as this provides a finer point. When base is started and spokes are
bent almost double at their centers to form the point, weave
upward to 1½ inches from center.

Sides—Cut sixteen bi-spokes of No. 4 reed 18 inches long and insert on left side of each of the old spokes, pushing new spokes down about 1½ inches into former weaving. With the hands, shape the point as desired, with uprights bending upward and outward. Change to No. 2 reed. With two strands, weave Pairing Weave over groups of two spokes, until 2½ inches from center. Trim off old weavers. Take three strands of No. 3 weavers, insert

DESIGNS FOR SIMPLE WATERTIGHT CONTAINERS

one each behind three consecutive pairs of spokes, and weave Triple Weave for five or six rounds, about 1½ inches.

Now separate pairs of spokes into single spokes, still continuing Triple Weave with No. 3 weavers. Push well down between spokes while separating. Weave 1 inch more of Triple Weave. You have now woven about 6 inches up from the base. Stop Triple Weave above the spokes exactly where it started, and cut off spokes on inside of basket.

Next, weave with flat winding reed for 3 inches. Use Japanese Weave with one weaver, and start by inserting weaver behind the last spoke where Triple Weave stopped. Continue weaving over two spokes and back of one for 2½ inches, then turn spokes in slightly for curve near top and weave ½ inch more. Cut off flat weaver behind spoke at which it started. Insert three new No. 3 weavers for Triple Weave, starting the first one at this same spoke. Weave 2 inches more of Triple, gradually bringing basket into the graceful shape shown.

Border—Soak spokes and nip off every third one close to the weaving. Lay each spoke back of the spoke at its right and bring to the outside. Continue all around; bring last spoke back of the first one.

For the second round bring each spoke in front of the spoke at its right and to the inside. Bring last spoke over first one. Repeat this round once more. Clip off spokes on inside.

Ring Loop and Handle—For the ring, take on strand of No. 3 reed and soak until pliable. Make it into a ring 2 inches in diameter by twisting the reed around itself as many times as necessary to use two-thirds of its length. Run the reed between the grooves of each previous round. Use last third of reed for wrapping or locking over the ring.

For twisted handle, take two strands of well-soaked No. 4 reed, 5 feet long. Lay these strands together and twist tightly until they can be easily folded double at their centers. Push twisted handle thus made, up through ring. Fasten the twist temporarily just below the ring. The four ends must now be woven firmly into the border at the top of the basket. Insert awl under the border where the first end will come; insert end, and with the aid of the awl, lace it in and out of the spokes just beneath border for a distance of 4 inches until it is safely fastened. Repeat with the other strand on the same side, and with the two strands on opposite side of the basket. The strands must be fastened well into the border, since this insures a firm hold and makes the basket strong enough to be used for a potted plant with its heavy burden of earth. These ends can also be bent back and fastened for a second reversed row of interlacing. A handle can never be attached too firmly.

STAINING AND DECORATING

Use one package of seal brown commercial dye. This package should give twelve hanging baskets three dippings each. Mix and stir thoroughly into $\frac{1}{2}$ cup of cold water, using a porcelain container for mixing. Over this mixture pour 1 gallon of boiling water. Stir thoroughly. Dip the basket while the solution is hot, making sure that every part of it, including the handle, is immersed. Hang up to dry. Repeat the dipping process twice, three dippings in all, drying the basket thoroughly each time.

On the part of the basket made by the flat reed, you may stencil a bright little border after the basket is dry. Paint this with oil color or enamel. When border is dry, add a shellac finish.

FLAT WALL BASKET FOR VINES (*page* 97)

A hanging basket adds grace to a window, and there is no better place for vines or flowers than in the sunshine offered there.

MATERIALS

Base—One plywood base, $\frac{3}{16}$ inch thick, 8 inches long, 3 inches wide, cut to shape shown at *A*. Bore an uneven number of holes for No. 3 reed, $\frac{1}{4}$ inch from edge.

Spokes—No. 3 reed, 14 inches long.

Weavers—No. 2 reed.

Handles—Two strands No. 5 reed, 30 inches long.

STEPS IN WEAVING

Base and Sides—Soak spokes well. Insert into holes of base, leaving 3 inches of reed below base. Turn each end over the end at its right (shown at *A*). Stand basket upright (as at *B*), and start weaving with two strands No. 2 reed. Insert these strands behind a spoke (as at *C*) and weave together as if one. Pass reeds under the first spoke, over the second, and so on, all around. On the second round, the odd number of spokes makes the weavers alternate with their former positions, and the weaving continues this way. Piece separate weavers (shown at *D*). Make basket 4 inches high.

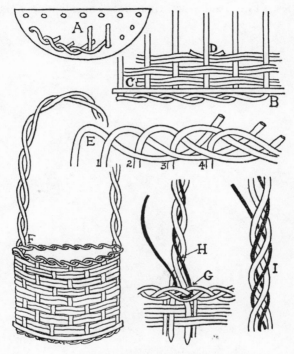

FLAT WALL BASKET FOR VINES

Border—Soak well before putting on border (shown at *E*). Each spoke passes behind the first one at its right: Spoke 1 passes in front of the next two, Spokes 2 and 3, and behind 4, and so on.

Handles—Whittle ends to a point, insert into weaving at back corner of basket (*F*); twist around each other, then insert in back at other side. To hold handles securely, a well-soaked strand of No. 2 reed is bent double and put through border (as at *G*); the two ends of it are run along in the two grooves made by the No. 5 reeds. One groove is shown filled by one of the ends (at *H*). The two grooves are filled (at *I*). At the other end fasten the No. 2 reeds very securely in the weaving, winding them back and forth many times. The handle will then hold considerable weight.

CHAPTER 15

THREE UNUSUAL PROJECTS

BASKET BIRDHOUSE (page 100)

THE FOLLOWING directions are for a birdhouse 9 inches high from base to top loop at peak, and 5 inches from base to ridge. The entrance opening is $1\frac{1}{2}$ inches high and as wide as the space between two spokes. The diameter of the house is determined by the size of its wooden base, which is listed under materials. The spokes of the watershed top extend beyond the walls of the house.

MATERIALS

Base—Round wooden base $8\frac{1}{8}$ inches in diameter, with fourteen holes bored $\frac{1}{2}$ inch from outer edge, for No. 5 reed.

Spokes—Fourteen uprights of No. 5 reed, 12 inches long, for birdhouse before roof is added. Six spokes of No. 4 reed, cut 20 inches long, and twelve spokes, 10 inches long, for separate watershed top. Additional spokes if necessary.

Weavers—Use $\frac{1}{2}$-inch flat reed to weave around sides, No. 2 reed for peak of watershed roof, No. 3 reed for remainder of roof.

Peak—Have a piece of tin made cone shaped, with soldered edges and with a diameter at its base of the same measurement as the diameter of the basket sides at the ridge where they join the roof. Leave an opening 1 inch in diameter at top. Use green or red metal paint to coat the tin peak on both sides to prevent rusting.

WEAVING AND FINISHING

Base and Sides—Insert the fourteen spokes or uprights 2½ inches below base. Pass each end over the end at its left and to inside

A BIRDHOUSE

(page 69). Then with a well-soaked ½-inch flat weaver, weave ten rounds of Under-and-Over Weave. The first part must be woven so as to leave an opening for an entrance as follows: Start reed at back of house, weave to front, reverse around spoke at one side of door, go completely around to other side, reverse, and continue for a height of 1½ inches. Remember that the reed used in reversing must be well soaked. Weave completely around basket to a height of 5 inches from the base.

Peak—Turn uprights inward, bring to a peak, and tie. Slip painted cone-shaped tin down over peak of spokes. Leave spokes of base tied until you finish weaving the watershed top.

Watershed top—Use six spokes of No. 4 reed, 20 inches long. Pierce holes in three spokes and run other spokes through these to form button or peak. With No. 2 reed, weave around these four groups of crossed spokes with Pairing Weave. Make cup-shape and weave for 1 inch. Now slip cup down over group of spokes from birdhouse base part, so that group of spokes will be at one side of point. Twist these base spokes into a loop 2 inches in diameter to make a ring handle from which to hang the birdhouse. Fasten down the ends of ring handle underneath watershed top.

Continue weaving this top, using No. 3 reed and Pairing Weave over pairs of spokes for ½ inch more. Now split into single spokes; add a new spoke 10 inches long beside each old spoke. Weave over the new pairs. Widen out top. Add more spokes if needed.

The top at its widest point should coincide with top of walls of base section. Tie down to walls. Leave spokes uncut to make an overhanging roof.

HANDY TRAY OF REED OR CREPE PAPER
(*page* 102)

A tray is useful—in the hall for cards, on the bureau for cuff links or jewelry, and on the desk for rubber bands and paper clips.

MATERIALS

This practical tray requires only a few ends of reed and a wooden base. Smaller and simpler trays may be planned, using for a base several pieces of smooth cardboard glued together and put under a press, with holes for wire spokes made by an awl. Weave with crepe-paper rope.

STEPS IN WEAVING

Base—Make a circle of wood (*A*) $\frac{3}{16}$ inch thick and 6 inches in diameter. Bore holes for spokes $\frac{1}{4}$ inch from edge, $\frac{3}{4}$ inch apart. (Such bases may also be bought at reed factories.) Cut spokes of No. 3 reed 10 inches long. Soak in water one hour; insert into holes of base with 3 inches protruding below board. To fasten, bend each spoke in succession over the end at its right, then bend in, as at *B*. Turn basket right side up.

Weaving Sides—Use No. 2 reed or crepe-paper rope narrower than the spokes. Soak reed until pliable. Bend weaving strand double, squeeze with pincers at center, and loop bent center around a spoke (*C*). Use Pairing Weave, twisting weavers over each other between spokes. Piece as shown at *D*. Make six rounds of Pairing. To produce flare in shape, bend spokes out gradually, then turn tray upside down on table with spokes radiating, as at *E*. Press down on tray to increase flare, and weave six more rows, twelve in all. Clip off weavers.

Border—Soak the spokes well by inserting only the top of the tray under warm water, keeping wooden or cardboard base dry. Shake off water. Then take any spoke, pass it under the first spoke to its right (see *F*), then over the second and third spokes, and in behind the fourth. Do this to each spoke all around the basket.

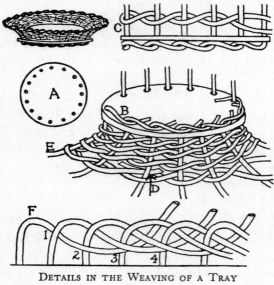

DETAILS IN THE WEAVING OF A TRAY

Now take the ends and slip each one over the end at its right and in (as shown at *B*). These are now firmly fastened.

To decorate inside of tray, paste in a picture and shellac it when shellacking tray. All must be thoroughly dry before shellacking either basket or picture.

If you prefer, paint a design on the wooden base, let it dry, and then shellac. Baskets having wooden bases are also attractive when not decorated but merely stained with wood stain after the tray has dried throughout. Shellac or wax will give a satisfactory finish.

A PACK BASKET

A pack basket is a very convenient piece of equipment for the outdoor enthusiast and may be made at home by basketry methods out of flat ash splints. Planned to fit the shape of the hiker's back, it is strong as well as flexible, causing no discomfort to the carrier, and is used for holding food and articles necessary for hiking and camping trips. The basket has a flat base and will stand alone on the ground. Web straps, sometimes reinforced with leather and which keep the pack balanced and neatly in place, may be used.

Splints for making the basket may be purchased from basketry supply houses or may be fashioned by the handy woodsman by hammering along an ash log in the traditional method. The strips of ash peel off readily after sufficient hammering. Heavier strips may be cut from hickory or oak. These can be shaped with a heavy sharp knife. All wood splints may be smoothed by scraping along their surfaces with the sharp edge of a knife.

MAKING THE BASKET

The splints measure from $\frac{1}{2}$ inch to $\frac{5}{8}$ inch wide. They should be well soaked before making the basket, to render them pliable. The base measures 8 inches by 18 inches. Weave the splints in and out of one another, as shown at *A*. Before turning up the spokes to make the sides, soak them well in water, then turn at a right angle, as at *B*, while a long, flexible splint is used to weave under and over successive splints to make the sides. There must be an odd number of upright splints in the sides to cause the proper alternation of the weaving splint. The corners of the basket may be reinforced by using heavier spokes at the four corners, as shown at *C*.

The basket may be made in the shape shown or to fit one's own particular needs, and its height when finished measures 18 inches. The flexible weaver keeps passing under and over the flat vertical spokes to make the attractive and practical basket surface. The opening at the top of the basket measures 6 inches wide and 14 inches long.

FINISHING THE TOP

The top is finished as shown in the detailed sketches, *D* to *G*. A round rod or piece of reed about $\frac{3}{8}$ inch in diameter is used as

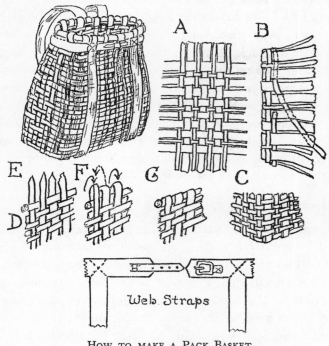

HOW TO MAKE A PACK BASKET
(Courtesy Scouting Magazine)

the last row, passing under and over the spokes at the top, as shown at *D*. These spokes are whittled to taper at their points, *E*. They are then soaked well and bent down over the round rod, where they pass down into the weaving beside a vertical spoke, as shown at *F* and *G*.

The basket may be shellacked, when finished, to render it more durable.

CHAPTER 16

MENDING AND PIECING

I N THE mending of reed baskets and similar products, divide the work into two parts: first, the mending of spokes, or uprights; and second, the mending of weavers.

MENDING SPOKES

In the mending of spokes, or uprights, trim new reeds into smooth points at ends. First insert the awl or a long, smooth wire to open the passage on the left side of the broken spoke. Move this awl or wire to the left, and insert the new spoke to the full length of the broken spoke. Then cut out and remove the broken spoke and push the new one into position.

If the spoke, or upright, is broken at the turn or edge between the side and base, two awls or wires must be used for insertion purposes—one for the base and one on the side. In this case, start a new upright from the top, and push it down through the side with enough length for threading into the base. Then, if using the reed, thoroughly soak and insert.

After the upright has been placed in position in the base, pull from the top in order to tighten it to the same tension as the other spokes. If necessary, finish top end of spoke by interlacing it into the stitches of the border.

MENDING THE BASIC WEAVES

MENDING SINGLE UNDER-AND-OVER WEAVE (*page 51*)

Allow short weaver to end behind the upright. Cut the weaver on the slant to the right of the upright, and by the use of an awl or wire, lay a new weaver back of the same upright. Then weave it in the same way as the other weavers to close the broken parts. Always trim on the left side of the upright.

MENDING DOUBLE UNDER-AND-OVER WEAVE (*refer to page 51*)

The mend for this double weave is performed like the single Under-and-Over Weave mend, except that the new weaver is always inserted below both old weavers, whether the broken end to be mended is the under or the upper weaver.

MENDING THE JAPANESE WEAVE (*page 51*)

Arrange the short weaver end behind the upright, and trim this weaver on the right side of the upright. Use an awl or wire, if necessary, to pry the weavers apart.

Insert the new weaver down into the weaving on the left side of the upright. Then bring the new weaver back of the same upright, on top of the short end, and to the outside of basket. Continue weaving until the broken parts are closed. In mending valuable pieces it is sometimes advisable to use the Triple Weave instead of the Japanese Weave in the mending of a Japanese weaver. The Triple Weave closes up the spaces smoothly.

MENDING THE DOUBLE JAPANESE WEAVE (*page 53*)

Follow same directions given in Under-and-Over Weave. Remember to insert a new weaver below the weaver to be repaired, when either the upper or under part is to be mended.

MENDING PAIRING WEAVE (*page 56*)

Mending Pairing Weave is done exactly the same way as the Under-and-Over Weave except that the weavers are carried in pairs.

Mending Triple Weave (*review page 56*)

Locate the mending spoke (the spoke at point of mending), and trim the weaver to be mended about $\frac{1}{4}$ inch on right side of this spoke. Squeeze this weaver with pincers, or nip it slightly on left side of mending spoke, then turn it down into the weaving at left of same spoke.

Use an awl or wire to open a place to insert a new weaver in the basket on the right side of next spoke at left of mending spoke. Point the end of new weaver, nip or squeeze it about 1 inch from end, then tuck it down 1 inch into the weaving at the right of this spoke. Now carry the new weaver back of the mending spoke and to the outside of the basket. This procedure insures a strong, smooth mend. This weave may be mended also by the Japanese method (No. 5).

Mending a Coil (*page 56*)

End the short old weaver back of an upright. This upright is called the mending spoke. Pull the weaver away from the upright to the inside of the basket. Then insert the new weaver at the right of the spoke to the left of the mending spoke. Carry the new weaver beside the old one so that it locks with it, then behind the mending spoke and to outside of the basket.

Mending an Arrow (*pages 53 and 59*)

Mend Arrow Weaves as you mend Coils.

CHAPTER 17

WEAVING WITH SUBSTITUTES

RETAILERS SELL many useful and beautiful articles of basket-weaving such as porch furniture, lamps, magazine racks, tea tables, market baskets, clothes hampers, plant stands, and wastebaskets. These are made by the same methods used in home weaving, with occasional use of wooden framework for the larger pieces. But the material used is different. Basket reeds are an imported product, and their cost is too great for the use of commercial companies making reed furniture on a large scale. Therefore, reed substitutes have been developed, and these have proved so practical that today we are beginning to use them for the hand weaving crafts. These substitutes are of the same size and appearance. They are used in the same way, and they cost less than imported reeds.

FIBER REED

One of the imitation reeds is called Fiber Reed. This imitation comes as a round strand, is made of pulp or fiber, and sometimes has a wire running through the center to give it added strength. It needs no soaking except when making sharp turns for borders, when it may be moistened slightly with a wet cloth and pinched with pincers at the bending point to prevent its breaking. For most purposes it is easily bent with the fingers. It comes in the same sizes as reed, starting at No. 1 ($\frac{1}{16}$ inch in diameter), through No. 6 ($\frac{5}{32}$ inch in diameter). It comes in a natural reed color or a little darker, takes shellac or paint, and costs half as much as imported reed.

ARTCRAFT FIBER CORD

Artcraft fiber cord is another imitation reed much softer than the fiber reed just described. This cord never requires soaking,

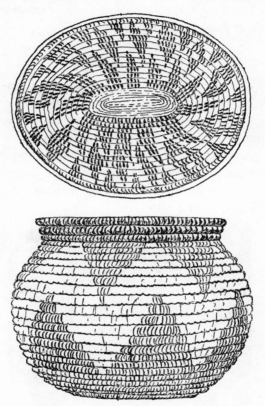

AN INDIAN BASKET TRAY AND GRAIN CONTAINER
These baskets may be made by sewing over imitation reed with raffia (see pages 134 and 145).

comes in sizes from $\frac{3}{32}$ to $\frac{5}{32}$ inch round, and costs about the same as the fiber reed. The fiber reed makes good spokes; the fiber cord, being softer, makes better weaving material.

IMITATION RUSH

Imitation rush is a heavy reed substitute used instead of genuine rush for chair seating or for basketmaking. It is round and tough, nearly $\frac{1}{4}$ inch in diameter, costs half as much as imported rush, and makes excellent material for spokes.

FLAT PAPER REED

There is a variety of paper reed sold in flat form—$\frac{1}{4}$, $\frac{3}{8}$, and $\frac{1}{2}$ inch wide. It is available plain, finished, and wax finished.

These reed substitutes may be used in place of genuine reed of the same size in weaving the products described in this book. Paper reed is usually packed in one-, two-, and three-pound cartons and is now more easily procured than imported reeds. Strands of cellophane may also be used as weaving material. Cellophane is made in various sizes and colors.

A Young Girl Designing Her Own Basket of Twisted Paper Reed

WEAVING WAMPUM BELTS

The American Indian has always been a skilled weaver. And the Wampum belt is a coveted Indian possession. It is made by stringing together small beads or light shells. Ingenious designs are worked into the belts with beads, shells, and seeds. These belts were once used not only for adornment but as a medium of exchange.

The commercial cords may be made successfully into all kinds of belts. The cord is available in many colors and sizes, and belt buckles may be purchased in every size and design.

The weaving stitches described in this book can be applied to the weaving of any kind of belt. Great care should be exercised in the selection of cord, and in the proper fastening of the ends of these cords to the buckle before the weaving or braiding processes are started.

Further suggestions on the braiding and weaving of belts and other products from reed substitutes may be secured from the supply houses.

CHAPTER 18

DECORATION, DYES, STAINS, AND PAINTS

WEAVERS OF baskets, trays, bowls, and furniture should know something about the use of dyes, stains, and paints relating to the decorative side of the craft. First, study the kind of color material needed to get the best effects in color harmony, as well as the best results from a lasting finish. An art teacher, painter, or interior decorator might be asked for advice or instructions in this practical and important part of your weaving program. Every artist who uses the brush is proud of his profession, and is usually glad to impart information and discuss his science or art.

There is genuine stimulation in taking up the finishing of woven products, and in planning the proper dyeing and staining of different articles. The artist makes a careful study of color and color mixtures, and usually tries out the various combinations to secure a desired shade. You can buy at the drugstore solid extracts of vegetable dyes, out of which you may mix dyes for your own use. Keep a pair of rubber gloves and an enamel preserving kettle for use in mixing dyes. For mixing and dyeing, ordinary vessels such as saucepans, basins, crocks, china, or glass may be used. Articles should be brushed with soap, or with soda and water, and thoroughly rinsed before being dyed. A secret of success lies in boiling the dye slowly and leaving the articles in the dye for hours. Deep and permanent colors are produced in this way.

If you use the ready-mixed dyes and paints, the instructions on the packages should be carefully followed. Here are some suggestions for the making of the natural dyes.

HOME-MIXED DYES AND STAINS

Dyes made at home are practical and economical. They provide soft-toned colors and teach the use of materials found in nature. For lighter colors, additional water may be added after the first mixture has been prepared.

DARK RED. Use $\frac{3}{4}$ teaspoon of logwood extract, $\frac{1}{4}$ teaspoon of fustic extract, 2 tablespoons of cochineal, 2 tablespoons of stannous chloride, $\frac{1}{4}$ teaspoon of cream of tartar. Mix in a quart of water and boil slowly for several hours.

ORANGE. Mix in a quart of water: 1 tablespoon of orange fustic, $\frac{1}{4}$ teaspoon of cochineal, 2 tablespoons of stannous chloride, and $\frac{1}{4}$ teaspoon of alum. Boil slowly until the color is a trifle deeper than desired. This color becomes lighter as it dries out.

YELLOW BROWN. Boil the woven product for several hours in a solution of the following: 1 tablespoon of cutch extract and 1 tablespoon of fustic mixed in a quart of water.

OLIVE BROWN. Mix in a quart of water: 1 tablespoon of cutch extract, 1 tablespoon of fustic, and $\frac{1}{4}$ teaspoon of logwood. The product should be boiled slowly for several hours in this solution.

BROWN. Dissolve in 1 quart of water 2 tablespoons of madder. Place over a slow fire to simmer, but not to boil. Leave the material or basket in this solution for five or six hours. Keep the temperature just below the boiling point.

INDIAN RED. Boil the product for six hours in the following solution: 2 tablespoons of cutch extract and a small crystal of bluestone about the size of a dime, dissolved in a quart of boiling water.

GREEN. This green is made chiefly from indigo and fustic. Dampen the material to be dyed in a solution made by dissolving 3 ounces of alum in a quart of water. Then dye the product in the following solution: 1 tablespoon of indigo and a small crystal of copperas, in a quart of water. Leave in solution until the desired color depth has been obtained. Then rinse off the loose dye and put the article into a fustic bath consisting of 1 quart of water and 1 tablespoon of fustic. Instead of fustic, bark extract may be used. If a brighter shade is required, add 1 or 2 tablespoons of alum mordant. (Mordant is a solution of alum and water that makes the dye adhere to the product.)

OLIVE GREEN. Soak the product for half an hour, first in water, then in a solution made of 1 quart of water and 1 teaspoon of copperas. Boil in a solution made of a tablespoon of bark extract, $\frac{1}{2}$ teaspoon of indigo, and $\frac{1}{4}$ teaspoon of logwood dissolved in a quart of water.

DARK BLUISH-GREEN. Soak the material in a solution made of 1 teaspoon of copperas dissolved in a quart of water. Allow it to remain for half an hour. Then soak it in a fresh bath made of 1 quart of water in which has been dissolved 1 tablespoon of bark extract, $\frac{3}{4}$ tablespoon of indigo, and a small piece of logwood extract the size of a pea. Simmer this solution for several hours until you get the required shade. If you want a lighter color, use 2 quarts of water instead of 1.

HEDGEROW DYES

In ancient England, hedgerow dyes were often used for coloring purposes. The leaves of almond, peach, or pear trees were used. These leaves make green shades if they are boiled with alum and tartar.

A product dyed in king's blue, well scoured and then boiled with four parts of alum and one of tartar, makes a fine deep green. The article should be boiled for two hours in a liquor made from the root of sharp-pointed dock. This root grows in every hedge and field. It produces an infinity of shades from a straw color to an olive hue.

YELLOW. Use the roots of thoroughly dried yellow dock broken
into small pieces. Wash and soak for several days in 1 quart of
water in which ½ tablespoon of washing soda has been dissolved.
Boil material slowly for four or six hours. Strong shades of yellow
will result. To lighten the color add a little alum.

OLIVE BROWN. Use two pounds of fresh black walnut bark to
2 tablespoons of washing soda and a cup of rock alum. Cover these
with boiling water. The material should boil in this solution for
twenty-four hours. Stir and turn material, and add more water to
prevent dye material from boiling dry. After boiling, rinse in cold
water.

YELLOW BROWN. Soak one pound of oak bark in 1 quart of
water with a lump of washing soda the size of an egg. The product
should soak in this solution from three to six days. The material
should be washed in water containing soda, and boiled with the
oak bark until the desired shade of brown has been obtained. By
adding alum the color can be lightened.

COMMERCIAL DYES AND STAINS

The simplest method for finishing a woven product is to dip it
into a vessel of commercially prepared dye, dry thoroughly, and
finish with shellac. Any of the good standard dyes may be used as
dips for staining baskets. Use a porcelain or enamel pan or vat
and mix the dye with water, following directions on the package.
Dip each article three times, but allow it to dry thoroughly after
each dipping. The dipped article should be finished with a coat of
shellac. It is also possible to boil in the standard boiling dyes
articles that do not have wooden bases. Follow directions on the
package for dyeing cloth, but use half as much water for the reed
articles. Reeds may also be boiled in dyes and the dye set permanently before weaving.

If you wish to decorate an article by painting or stenciling, you
can do so after shellacking. Many articles will look better if no

stains are used, but if instead two or three coats of white shellac are given. Decorative articles look well stained with seal-brown packaged dyes, with handles stained in orange color, dark green, or coral dye. Many beautiful effects can be secured by staining or painting reeds or spokes, and then drying them before the article is woven. In first using paints and water colors it is necessary to learn the fundamentals of mixing and using them, and the method of applying them to different kinds of surfaces.

HOW TO MIX PAINTS

Mix black and white to get gray.
Mix yellow and blue to get green.
Mix red and yellow to get orange.
Mix red and blue to get violet.

The various tints and shades of gray, yellow, blue, red, green, violet, and orange are obtained by a variation in the mixture, using more or less of the basic color.

In the further study of dyes, stains, and paints, you may secure samples illustrating the use of color from a hardware dealer or a drugstore. Ask for catalogues of dyes and stains that illustrate not only the colors, but describe how they are used on different kinds of materials and products, and explain the process to be used on the kind of product that you wish to color. As a weaver you will do well to study a prismatic color diagram, the effect of color upon different articles, and the methods used to mix all kinds of color products in order to acquire other colors, shades, and tints.

PART III

Constructive Weaving Crafts

CHAPTER 19

HOW TO MAKE ROPE AND
TASSELS BY HAND

HOW TO MAKE ROPE (page 120)

As "GREAT oaks from little acorns grow," large ropes grow out of the tiniest of fibers twisted together. Alone a single fiber amounts to nothing, but when bound tightly with many fibers like itself, it becomes strong and unbreakable.

Ropemaking is simple, and anyone can make a heavy rope out of simple strands of twine or cord. By twisting together strands of floss you may obtain a large ropelike product of pleasing appearance. Such homemade ropes brighten the edges of various articles —collars, table scarves, pillows, or tie-backs for curtains. Ropes of cord take the place of ribbons for bows at the neck and for gay hat ornaments, shirred bags, apron cords, strings for pencils, or decorative ropes for mirrors or pictures. These ropes can be made in any size or color, or with several colors wrapped around each other, like stripes on a stick of peppermint candy.

To make a rope, first decide on the length you want. Then measure off two or three times this amount and cut several strands of cord of the same length. Tie these together in a knot at one end and slip over a hook (page 120, *A*). Grasp the other end of the strands between the fingers and twist, holding taut. Twist the strands round and round until they begin to kink, then fold double (as at *B*), taking the center of the fold in one hand, and the other two ends in the other. Twist them in the opposite direction (*C*).

A rope will result, double the size of the bulk of strands used in
starting; so in making any rope, begin with half the amount of
bulk desired for the final thickness.

Ropes over 3 feet in length should be made by two persons, for
a single pair of hands cannot stretch between the two ends. Let

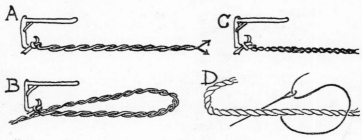

STEPS IN THE MAKING OF ROPE

each person twist at one end, then double the center around a
chair or bedpost, while one of the workers gradually slips along the
rope to this new second end. Each should slip in the opposite
direction, gradually slipping to this second end as the work pro-
gresses. Fasten the ends in a knot to keep them from untwisting.
To attach cord, stitch along lines of twist (*D*).

HOW TO MAKE TASSELS (*page* 121)

Tassels are used for the corners of mats, ends of bell pulls, bag
cords, sandal straps, belts, curtain tie-backs, and bookmarks. You
can make a tassel without using needle and thread. This is said to
be the method that sailors use.

Wind thread for tassel around palm of hand. Slip a loop of cord
around the top or head of the tassel (*A*, Sketch 1, page 121). This
is a colorful cord made by hand, as described earlier. Now hold
tassel in right hand with the lower end (*B*) between thumb and
fingers. With left hand, wind the thread chosen for the collar.
Make a loop of this near the top (as at *C*).

With left hand wrap cord around for collar (*D*, Sketch 2), leaving loop (*E*) long enough to be uncovered, and end (*F*) also uncovered. Wind close to each former round. When the collar

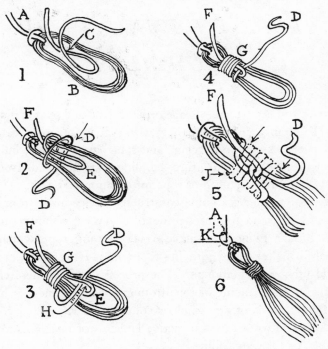

STEPS IN THE MAKING OF A TASSEL

(*G*) is the desired width (Sketch 3) put end *D* through loop *E* (as at *H*). Draw *H* entirely through, then pull upward on *F*. This draws end *D*, as well as loop *E*, up under collar to secure fastening (Sketch 4). An enlarged drawing at *J* (Sketch 5) shows interlocking loops under collar. Cut off ends *F* and *D* flush with collar (see arrows).

Tie tassel to corner of fabric (*K*, Sketch 6) by the two ends of fastening cord (*A*). Tie securely, then fasten both ends into fabric. Comb out tassel; trim even (Sketch 6).

CHAPTER 20

ROPE WEAVING WITH EQUIPMENT

T HE UNIVERSAL use of rope on both land and sea for first-aid, lifesaving, and emergency work, gives practical value to ropemaking, knot tying, and splicing. Farmers, builders, truckmen, handlers of furniture, building materials, and structural steel—all are in daily need of rope information and skill.

The rope twister is a home-constructed device made from three pieces of pine wood and three pieces of heavy wire (shown on page 123). Binder twine will make a very strong rope which can be used for halter ropes, jumping ropes, knot-tying work, or first-aid and lifesaving equipment. The process described here can be used also in the weaving of rope from strands of leather, or by the use of finer cords of any kind or color. The variegated colored strands can be woven into attractive lanyards or necklaces to hold pendants, or for watch fobs.

Ropemaking consists of two separate processes: First, the twisting together of several strands to form the initial length of rope; second, the doubling of this length of rope and its further twisting to lock the strands together in the final coil.

CONSTRUCTION OF EQUIPMENT

Step 1. The equipment needed for the first step will be: two boards (page 123, *A*), three hooks (*B*), these assembled (as at *C*), and a post (*D*) assembled with strands of twine (as at *E*).

Select two pieces of straight pine boards measuring 4 by 15 inches

(*A*). Bore three holes in each, the outside holes 3 inches from the ends and the center hole halfway between the others.

Take three pieces of wire, 8 inches long, of the size used for galvanized farm-fence wiring or wire coat hangers, and twist these

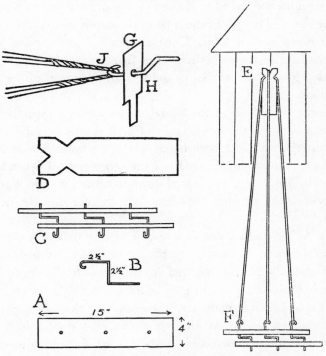

HOMEMADE ROPE TWISTER AND METHOD OF USING IT

into the shape of a crank (as at *B*). Allow 3 inches of crank length, $2\frac{1}{4}$ inches for the hook-end axle to be threaded through the hole of the shaft, and 3 inches for the other straight axle. Insert the three hooks (*B*) into the three respective holes of the pine boards (*A*), forming the twister (shown at *C*).

Make a binding post (*D*) out of pine board 4 by 10 inches, and cut out V-shaped notches at the top and two sides. Fasten this post to a tree or to the side of a barn or wall (as at *E*). The post can also be held firmly by a second person. The strands of twine or cord to be twisted are fastened to its notches (shown in Sketch *E*). The worker stands at the other end and turns the twister round and round to make the initial three-strand rope.

The size and length of the rope to be woven will be determined by the use to be made of it. Cut the strands about $2\frac{1}{2}$ times longer than the length of rope desired. The diameter of the rope may be increased by the use of two or more strands, instead of one, over each hook.

Tie the three ends of the strands to be wound, respectively, to the three hooks of the twister (as at *F*). A second person can hold the twister firmly with both hands while you fasten the strands of twine over the binding post (*E*) at the other end. Then take the twister in your own hands and turn it around to the right, or clockwise, thus twisting the three strands into one tight, thick strand.

Step 2. To make a double-strength rope by means of the single paddle (shown at *G*, page 123), the twisted rope just made may be folded over double and twisted in the opposite direction. This paddle is made of a piece of pine board measuring 4 by 10 inches. Bore a hole $\frac{1}{8}$ inch in diameter in the center of the upper, or board, end. Make a hook (like that shown at *B*) out of $\frac{1}{8}$-inch wire, having the same dimensions as those used for the three-strand twister. Insert this wire hook into the paddle board (as at *H*), with the hook on one side and the crank on the opposite side. This device is called a single twister. The lower part of the paddle is cut out to the shape of a handle to make it easy to hold in the left hand, while the right hand turns the wire crank to wind the rope.

Remove the three-strand rope from the hooks of the twister, and tie the ends in a knot. Leave the other ends attached to the post on the wall. Hook the center of the length of twisted rope over the hook of the single twister (as at *J*). Lay the ends of rope, taken from the twister, parallel to the rest of the rope, and attach it to the binding post beside the other ends already there. Now hold the paddle (*G*) in the left hand and turn the crank (*H*) with the right hand, counter-clockwise, or to the left, instead of to the right as for three-strand formation. This binds the two folded sections of rope together in a rope of double thickness. As soon as the rope begins to kink when twisted further, remove from poster notches and from the paddle (*G*) and tie knots in both ends. The making of the rope is now finished. This final rope is composed of six strands and is double the thickness of the initial twisted rope of three strands (in Step 1). This same method can be used to make a two-strand rope out of any two strands or twines.

GROUP SUGGESTIONS

An exhibit of ropemaking may be interesting for class or club demonstration, and can be staged in connection with special programs of class, school, club, or group. If two are to make up the demonstration team, the work should be divided, so that both are busy every minute in the preparation of material, making and setting up the device, and in the demonstration of the making of different sizes and lengths of rope, chains, or lanyards. The worker should practice until able to do the work skillfully and to turn out a substantial product. Give out samples to the audience and ask them to examine these. One of the demonstrators should give an oral explanation while the demonstration is under way. The project may be developed with a view to learning how to tie all kinds of rope knots, making rope splicings, and using the rope in the many practical ways common to the needs of industrial vocations and first-aid and lifesaving work of the community. A visit to the hardware store, department store, and other places where cords, string, twine, and rope are sold, will give valuable information about ropemaking.

CHAPTER 21

ARTICLES MADE OF ROPE
OR RAFFIA

PLANT CONTAINER OF RAFFIA KNOTS (page 127)

FILLED WITH a green vine, this openwork basket of knotted raffia or crepe-paper rope adapts itself to the winter window. The container is made very simply of strands knotted together, and requires less than two hours to complete.

MATERIALS

Twelve heavy strands of raffia or paper rope (natural or colored).

Six dark-colored oval beads, six light-colored oval beads, three dark-colored round beads, three light-colored round beads.

One pottery bowl about 5 inches high, 5 to 6 inches across.

MAKING THE BASKET

1st round. At the very bottom of the basket is a large knot. To make this, knot all the strands of rope or raffia together (as at *A*). Now mark points on all strands 3½ inches above the knot (see arrows). Make knots at these points, using two strands for each. This makes six knots (as at *B*). To string on the beads, moisten the ends of the strands and twist tightly to slip them through the holes. Push each pair of strands through a hole (as at *C*) to complete the first round of six knots and beads (*B, C*). The colors of the beads should alternate.

2nd round. Again mark points on each strand 3½ inches above

bead. For next knot, take one of these strands and the strand
next to it from its adjacent knot, and combine in a knot. Continue
thus all around basket, making six knots midway between knots of
first row (as at *D*). Slip an oblong bead above each knot (as at *E*),
alternating the colors.

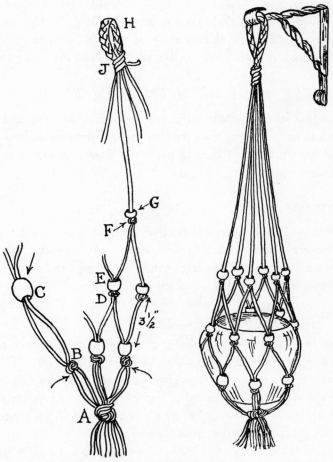

PLANT CONTAINER HELD IN KNOTTED NETWORK OF RAFFIA

3rd round. Again measure 3½ inches above last row of beads, split pairs, and make each knot from a strand of one pair and a strand of an adjacent pair. Make knots all around basket, six knots midway between knots of second row (as at *F*). Slip a round bead above each knot, alternating a light and a dark (as at *G*).

Top of Basket—Leave 12 inches plain above last row. Divide strands into three equal groups for a braid. Braid tightly for 6 inches (*H*). Bend braid over in a 3-inch loop. Wrap the ends of rope or raffia around beginning of braid in a tight collar (as at *J*), threading ends under collar with a needle to make secure.

BASKET MADE OF TWISTED PAPER (*page* 129)

For baskets once made with imported reed, we now use such American substitutes as fiber reed, or crepe paper twisted into rope. These substitutes were used to make the flower basket illustrated on the next page.

MATERIALS

Spokes—Twelve pieces of flexible wire, 20 inches long.

Weavers—Rope made of crepe paper (as in Chapter 20). Cut sections 1 inch wide across crepe-paper roll; twist and stretch until it forms a firm rope. Use single or double (*A*).

TO WEAVE BASKET

Lay two groups of six spokes each at right angles to each other. Fasten at center with a fine wire; bend out in pairs (*B*). To start weaving, split a pair, and put weaver between these two spokes (*C*). Weave under and over all pairs, but leave these two spokes single to get an uneven number of units for one weaver. This procedure provides for its alternation in successive rows.

Weave 1 inch; separate spokes into singles, as at *D*. Cut out one spoke (arrow) to get an odd number again. Make base 5 inches

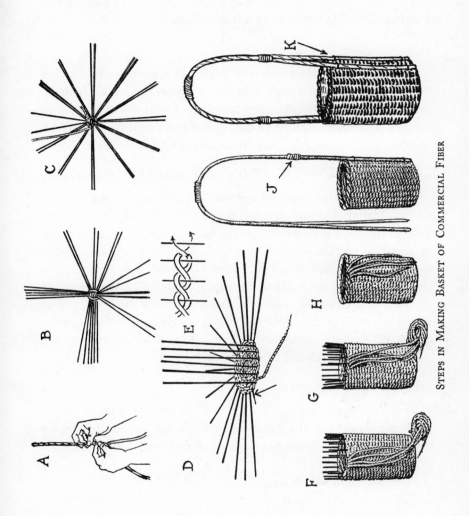

STEPS IN MAKING BASKET OF COMMERCIAL FIBER

in diameter. Then bend spokes upward; weave as high as desired. For heavier effect use Pairing Weave (shown at *E*).

BORDER AND HANDLE

At top, add a pair of weavers; use the two pairs in Pairing Weave twisted around spokes in heavy border. Bend each spoke over last stitch (*F*, *G*, *H*). For handle, cut two pieces of wire of a heavy size, wrap with crepe paper, and bend over basket. Wrap together at intervals (*J*). Attach to basket separately (as at *K*).

NAPKIN RING OF KNOTTED RAFFIA (*page* 132)

Just a single knot repeated again and again may result in a mesh fabric. Hammocks and net containers may be made in this way. One of the most popular and useful knots is the Square Knot (*A*). A variation of this, using four strands instead of two in tying, is known as King Solomon's Knot (*B–G*). You can use either of these knots to make a tied raffia napkin ring. The same method of tying knots may be used to make a belt or a mesh bag. The following project shows the use of King Solomon's Knot, with colors to produce attractive stripes. There is opportunity for originality in your choice of color.

MATERIALS REQUIRED

Raffia or some strong flexible cord in one or several colors. (Colors used in ring illustrated are: two outside groups, producing four strands each, green; groups next to these, orange; center group is natural.)

A bread board to work on.

Thumbtacks and cord.

Some shellac.

STARTING THE KNOT

Soak raffia well; squeeze nearly dry in a towel. Stretch a cord

(B) across a board, knot ends, and fasten down with tacks. For first knot, loop two strands of raffia at their centers; place the loop up behind the cord (as at C). Bring ends through loop (D). Pull taut (E). Make five loops over cord in this way, leaving twenty raffia ends for tying.

TYING THE KNOT

To make this knot, take two strands from end group and two from next group, making four strands in a row—*a, b, c, d*.

For *first part of knot* (F), knot *a* and *d* around *b* and *c*, with *d* entirely over *b* and *c*, and *a* under them (as shown at F).

For *second part of knot* (G), take left strand, which is now *a*, and lay it under *b* and *c*. Loop one around the other as shown, finishing knot. (Double lines represent a single strand.) Pull knot up snugly (as shown at H).

For each knot, take two from one group and two from group at its right. For next row of knots, take two strands at right of each knot, such as *a'*, *b'*, and place with two at left of next knot, as *c'*, *d'*. Repeat across.

At sides, leave two extra strands untied in every other row, bringing into knot at next row (as shown at I, page 132).

For section of complete mesh, see H. Knot 6 or 7 inches of mesh, then bring ends of the last row of knots down through loops of the first row, and tie in overhand knot (J). Repeat all across. Put a piece of raffia in place of the first cord (B) stretched across board, and fasten under ring (see arrow, J).

Slip ring over a tumbler to dry in circular form. Shellac ring when dry.

Tie Square Knot in the same way, but omit central strands to tie over.

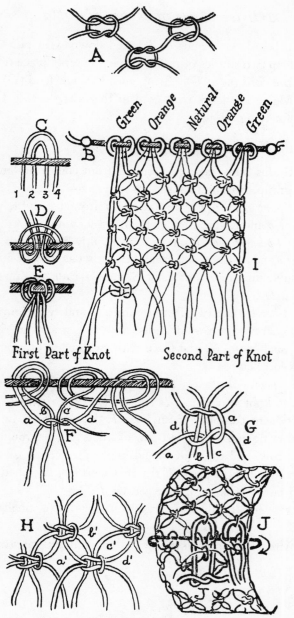

First Part of Knot

Second Part of Knot

KNOTTED RAFFIA TO MAKE NAPKIN RING, WITH DETAILS OF
SQUARE KNOT AND KING SOLOMON'S KNOT

GIFT NOVELTIES MADE OF RAFFIA (*page* 134)

Sewing on canvas with raffia is a craft that will appeal to many. In the purses and bags shown in the illustration there is a chance to combine the soft waxy raffia colors effectively. The purses shown at *A, B, C,* and *D* may be made by weaving with strands of raffia across carpet warp set at twelve threads per inch, then cutting the finished cloth to desired shape.

MATERIALS

Canvas with eleven to twelve holes per inch; blunt raffia or tapestry needles; natural raffia for background; waxed colored raffia for designs. The natural raffia should be soaked an hour or more in water, then wrapped in a damp towel while being used. Waxed colored raffia does not need to be soaked.

UNDERARM PURSE (*A*)

Cut canvas 16 inches long and 9 inches wide. Divide 16-inch length into three sections, 5, 6, and 5 inches wide, respectively. On check paper, make design to fill these spaces, but leave ¾ inch on all edges for turning under. Embroider the design solid with raffia, with the exception of the ¾ inch edge. Use vertical stitches like solid embroidery, or use the technique shown at *G.* Line with a piece of sateen the same size, turning edges under and overcasting sateen to canvas at edges. Put wooden peg button on center section. Make a loop at edge of lap to go over it. Background may be tan; design, turquoise and black, or rose and black.

CURVED UNDERARM PURSE (*B*)

Cut piece of canvas 10 inches horizontally and 8 inches vertically, as shown at sketch 4. Cut lower corners round. Cut another piece 10 inches horizontally and 12 inches vertically, 5 and 6. Cut 4 inches of the 12 into tabs, as at 6. Embroider with long

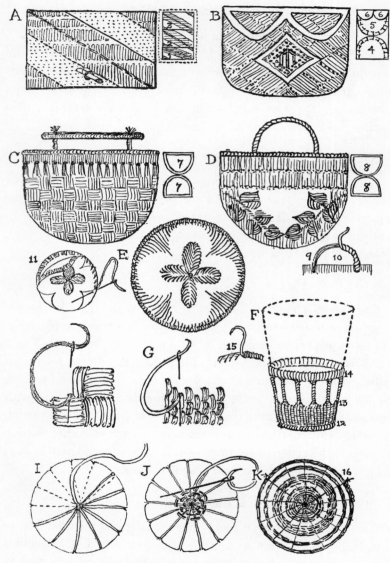

GIFT NOVELTIES MADE OF RAFFIA

raffia stitches in squares measuring 1½ inches. Cut ¾-margin at edge into tabs, and fold over as shown at 4 and 5. Line each section with sateen; then put sections together, overcasting edges; alternate squares, using two colors.

KNITTING BAG WITH WOOD HANDLE (*C*)

Make this bag of two pieces of canvas, 10 inches by 12 inches, cut to shape, as at 7. Roll top edges down; cover with button-holing. Add fringe of raffia. Make handles of two round dowels, each 10 inches long; bore ⅛-inch holes 1 inch from ends; then pull ropes of raffia through them and make knots at their ends.

SOFT-HANDLED KNITTING BAG (*D*)

This bag resembles bag *C*. Embroider the leaves with green against a natural background; make upper part rose or gold with a green border at top. Make handle by looping raffia several times across 6 inches at top of bag, as at 9; then wrap raffia around the strands, as at 10.

ROUND PLAQUE (*E*)

To make the plaque or vase mat, cut a circular piece of canvas; embroider in suitable design; clip ¾-inch edge into tabs; turn under and line, as at 11. Overcast edges.

GLASS HOLDER (*F*)

Make this holder of raffia woven over hat wire. Cut sixteen spokes of the wire, each 9 inches long. Make into a Japanese base, page 37. Weave around with raffia to edge of base; turn wires up as side spokes and weave around them for 1 inch, see 12 and 13. Now group wires into pairs, and warp around them with raffia for upright posts. At top separate into singles and weave ¼ inch, 14. Turn wires under diagonally, as at 15; overcast with raffia. Also overcast edge at base.

Hot Mat of Raffia (*I*, *J*, *K*)

This simple little raffia article makes a useful household gift. Measure a thick piece of cardboard 6 inches in diameter and make a hole at its center, as at *I*. Around the circumference, mark an odd number of equidistant points, about thirty-nine. (Only thirteen are shown in the illustration, for clarity.) Make a notch at each point; wrap round and round from center to each notch with carpet warp, as shown. Now sew in and out of the cord spokes with colored raffia, as at *J*. Use tan at center for about 1 inch; change to a dark color for $\frac{1}{2}$ inch; then $\frac{1}{4}$ inch tan; $\frac{1}{2}$ inch dark color; and so on until you have worked out an attractive spiral design of several colors, as at *K*. Weave close up to edge on first side; then turn cardboard over and weave a spiral design on second side. Leave cardboard enclosed between the two woven sides. When finished, overcast edges with raffia or make a border of buttonholing, as at 16.

CHAPTER 22

BRAIDING WITH FIBERS

BRAIDING WITH CORNHUSKS (page 139)

THERE IS always fascination in the discovery of new uses for old and native products. A few hours spent in the cornfield during husking time may result in acquiring a supply of variegated soft inner husks for weaving baskets, rugs, and mats.

Cornhusks are one of the strongest of weaving materials if selected, treated, and used correctly. And the weaver does not have to wait for funds and time to start weaving. Many weavers find or secure cornhusks near home and prepare them for use when needed.

Select the long, soft, lightly tinted inner husks, and separate these into piles based upon length and color.

Place the white husks by themselves. Then classify the tans, browns, and red tints to enable yourself to carry out a color scheme in weaving. When a single or uniform variety of cornhusk makes it impossible to obtain a natural selection of shades and tints, you may use commercial dyes to get the desired colors; or the husks may be used in their soft, natural colors.

After they have been seasoned and dried, store the surplus cornhusks in a cool place where they will not mildew. They will keep well when dropped loosely in paper bags and hung in a closet. Store different colors and tints in separate bags and mark each bag to indicate the color and length of husks.

Before using, the husks should be moistened and kept in a damp cloth or container for a few hours or overnight.

BRAID MAKING

Best results are obtained by weaving the husks into braids of different sizes. Therefore, a good introduction to cornhusk weaving is practice in making many kinds and sizes of braid. Begin by cutting or separating the husks into strips ranging from ½ to 1½ inches in width.

In weaving braids you should use assorted lengths of husks in order to maintain uniform strength and size of braid, and to prevent all ends from breaking at the same point. To start your first braid, take six strips of husks of different lengths and tie them firmly together at the stem ends; separate the strips into three strands of two pieces each, and begin braiding the three double strands. As you reach the near ends of the shortest strips, open up the ends and place the butt end of a new strip over these. Then by rolling or twisting slightly while braiding, continue in this way, concealing the rough places where the splices occur. By selecting husks of different lengths but of the same width, and continuing this splicing method, you can make a braid of uniform size throughout. Then by changing both size and number of strands, you may secure braids of any size and shape. See page 139, *A, B,* and *C.*

If you want a flat braid, the strands should be folded and woven flat. For a round braid, all strands must be rolled while braiding, using enough strands to make the braid round.

BRAIDED ARTICLES (*pages* 140 *and* 143)

Articles made of other braided materials such as raffia, cattails, and grasses, have a pleasant texture and soft color. The fibers must first be dried. Then they are soaked in water and laid in a damp towel for use. To color fibers, soak well and boil in dyes.

Sewing braids into circles produces hats, mats, round rugs, bags, and trays, and is done as follows (see page 139):

Step 1. Tie ten to fifteen strands of raffia or other material to a hook (as at *A*). Braid with three or five strands in each braid, adding new pieces as the old are consumed (*B*). Trim off the ends.

For cattails, use only one strand or rush for each part of braid.

Step 2. Wrap around the braid-end six times with a raffia strand (*C*). Thread other end of raffia through a large darning needle. Draw it under and around the first few wrappings (as at arrow) and pull taut.

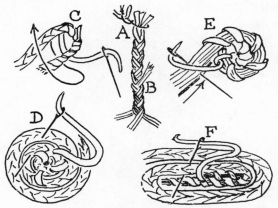

METHODS OF HANDLING BRAIDED MATERIAL

Step 3. Wind second row around circle thus made. Sew edges together (as at *D*). Sew one round after another, working on the wrong side. Instead of a braid, a bundle of grass fibers or a cattail leaf may be used (as at *E*), taking stitches with a sewing strand around the bundle into the last row. Add new fibers (as at arrow, *E*).

GARDEN HAT OF CORNHUSKS

This hat is shown on page 143. Sew a circle 6 to 8 inches wide for top of hat. Turn braid on edge to sew around sides. Sew on outside of hat, making sides 3 to 4 inches deep. For brim, turn braid horizontally and sew on other side. Line brim with bright chintz.

Make a round garden mat to kneel on to match the hat, and an oval bag (see page 143).

SANDALS

A braided sandal is cool and colorful and may be made of braided raffia, cornhusks, cattails, or long, fibrous grasses. A braid 10 feet long will make an 8-inch sandal. Tie fifteen strands of raffia at their ends, fasten to a hook (*A*), and make a three-strand braid with five strands of raffia in each of the braid units. Add new strands (*B*), and braid for 9 or 10 feet. For a mottled sandal, make one braid-unit of a different color.

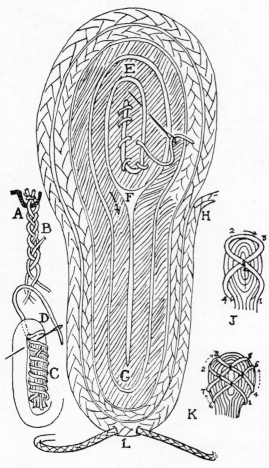

STEPS IN MAKING A SANDAL OF BRAIDED FIBERS

To sew the sandal, wrap the top end of braid with a raffia strand (shaded end, *C*); bend braid around wrapped part and start sewing together the adjacent edges (*D*). Make two rounds (*E*), then make a loop straight downward to heel (*F* to *G*) 4 inches long. Continue sewing braid around this foot shape for three or more rounds, according to your foot size, then fasten end at one side (*H*).

Two methods of attaching sandal straps are shown (at *K* and *J*, page 140). In each method, fasten end of braid (at *H*) and follow the numbers given, passing along the edge of the sandal at dotted lines. To tie sandal to heel, make a narrow cord or braid and insert it through heel (*L*). Tie up the ends around the ankle.

ROUND SEWING BASKET OF BRAIDS (page 142)

Base and Sides—In making a sewing or fruit basket, use braid of uniform size for sides and bottom. A satisfactory size for braids is $\frac{1}{2}$ inch wide and $\frac{1}{4}$ inch thick. The base must lie flat on a table. Start winding (page 139, *D*) by twisting braid around in a circle. Sew together successive rounds with strong waxed thread. When the base is 5 or 6 inches in diameter, start the sides by sewing the first side or base braid in an upright position to the last braid edge of the bottom, and continue to the desired height. The upper edge of the basket may have an extra braid sewed on top of the last braid. Do likewise with the bottom edge. The doubling of top and bottom will improve the appearance and give greater strength to the basket for handle support.

Handle—The handle of this basket is made by using two heavy braids and sewing them securely through double braids at top and bottom. A more attractive handle is made by using two braids and weaving them together across the top. They separate into a V-shape at both sides (as shown above).

BASKETS, MATS, AND RUGS

It is important to learn to make a good braid. Once you have

BASKET OF BRAIDED CORNHUSKS. THE BRAIDS ARE FLATTENED,
WITH DOUBLE BORDERS AT BASE AND BORDER

learned this technique, you can apply it to other articles. This braid can be worked readily into many interesting forms such as mats for electric irons, coffee urns, teapots, and for hot dishes for the table. A cornhusk mat for the kitchen or front door will save the floors and carpets from much dirt. From cornhusk braids you can also make rugs. The braids are simply shaped and sewed into oval, round, square, or rectangular strips.

BRAIDING WITH RAGS AND CLOTH

Weaving with uniform strips of rags and cloth is done in much the same way as with cornhusks. The rags can be made into braids, and from these braids are woven the mats, rugs and baskets.

By a combination of reed, spokes, and braids, made from either cornhusks or rags, many products besides baskets may be woven. The weaver uses a foundation of spokes, following the same directions as given in the chapters for making baskets with reed and raffia, substituting the cornhusks or rag braids for the strands of reed and raffia.

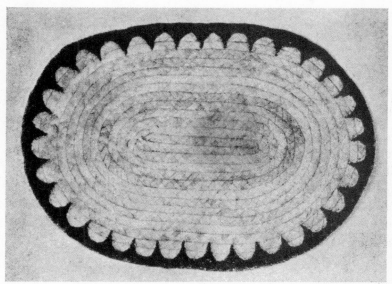

A Useful Foot Mat made of Heavy Clumps of Pine Needles, with Scallops Painted around Edge

Articles made from Braided Material

CHAPTER 23

USING NATURAL FIBERS

O VER A soft coil of gray-green grasses, the wood-brown of pine needles, or even the flexible inner leaves of yellow cornhusks, you may sew with raffia. Use fine bark strips or tufting cotton to make baskets for summer garden flowers. The very same method produces coasters and trays. The craft of sewn fibers is easy to learn and costs little. A circle 3 inches wide makes a coaster for a tumbler; when it widens to 6 inches it becomes a tray or base for the pitcher. And the same base may be continued and turned upward in a gradual curve to make the flower baskets shown here.

PINE NEEDLES FOR WEAVING

Gather pine needles in late spring or summer after they have grown to full size and before insects injure them. The best needles are those gathered from the tree itself, although the fallen needles that have turned brown may be used.

For *green needles*, dry the needles in the house or the shade away from the sun. For *brown needles*, leave out in the wind, sun, and rain. Turn needles frequently to dry evenly; if placed between two screens they dry nicely. Turn the screen over now and then for even drying. As the needles dry, the sheaths shrink and may be pulled from the clusters of needles.

When the right color is produced, dip needles in hot water to kill any insect eggs that may be on them. Dry thoroughly and keep dry until needed. Just before using, soak in water a few minutes, then wrap in a damp towel. Raffia or split roots for sewing should be soaked in a basin of water for fifteen minutes, shaken out, and then wrapped in a bath towel until each strand is needed.

STITCHES USED WITH PINE NEEDLES

BEGINNING THE STITCH

Wrap raffia around several clusters of the needles (*below*, *A*). Wind wrapped part around in a circle. Stitch the first round through the center. Continue second round, taking each stitch

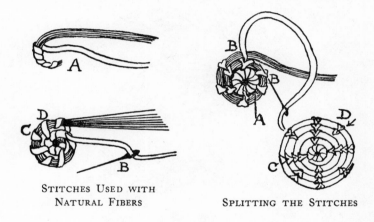

STITCHES USED WITH
NATURAL FIBERS

SPLITTING THE STITCHES

(*B*) through the stitch beneath it in the preceding round. Also stitch through the bundle of needles at the same time. Continue wrapping raffia once around coil (*C*), then stitching through last row (*D*). Space stitches carefully.

SPLITTING THE STITCHES

Make first and second round like plain stitch (*A* above). In the third round (Step 2), take each stitch through center of stitch just beneath it (*B*, *above*). As the rows progress, the stitches form radiating lines (*C*). As the space widens between these, start new

stitches between the first rows (*D*). Rows of stitches are about
1 inch apart.

Double Split Stitch *page* (145)

Start center as described above. Then take two stitches, instead
of one, through each hole, beginning at third round. Take regular

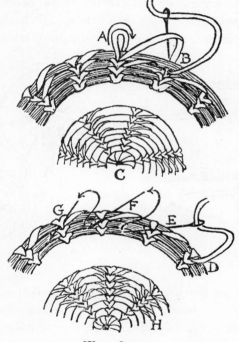

WING STITCH

stitch (*A*), then another stitch through the same hole (arrow *A*).
Proceed to right for next split stitch (*B*), and so on (see *C*).

Wing Stitch (*above*)

Complete one round of regular split stitch. At end of round
(*D*), reverse, and take single stitches in opposite direction (as shown

by successive stitches—*E, F, G*), which makes double wings (see *H*). When back to *D* again from other side, continue the next round with split stitch (*A, B*), then reverse.

PINE-NEEDLE PROJECTS (*page* 145)

The flower bowl (*right*) is made of a base of pine needles measuring 5 inches across (*A*), broadened to the diameter of 7 inches at *B*, where the coil is re-inforced with wire. Two extra ends are carried to top in manner of *D*. The basket is narrowed for the neck (*C*) to a width of 4 inches. The top row is reinforced.

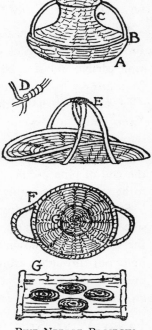

The flower basket (*right*) is made of a sewed circle of needles, 15 inches in diameter. When finished, it is wetted and reinforced with wire around the last row. Then it is bent into shape and dried. Handles are made of wires covered with wrapping (*E*).

The tray illustrated (*F*) is 10 inches wide, reinforced at outer row with a second row of wire added and extended at sides for handles. These handles must be wrapped.

The coasters (at *G*) are 3-inch circles and are easily made.

PINE-NEEDLE PROJECTS

POSTCARD TRAY WITH PINE-NEEDLE RIM
(*page* 149)

Picture postcards are just the right size and shape to make the bases of small trays, jewelry containers, or desk trays for odds and ends.

MATERIALS

A clump of pine needles ⅛ inch thick, to sew over. (Also suitable are heavy wrapping cord, or a piece of basketry reed.)

Some raffia or heavy Germantown yarn for sewing.

A blunt raffia or tapestry needle.

Stiff cardboard to give the postcard body.

Shellac to give a glossy coat when tray is finished.

MAKING THE TRAY (*page* 149)

With sharp scissors round off the four corners of the postcard. From a box or the back of a pad, cut a piece of firm cardboard the same shape and size, and round off corners like the card (*A*). Measure points all around the card ½ inch apart and ¼ inch from edge, and prick holes through these points with a sharp needle. Keep both cards evenly together. (Cards with pricked holes are shown at *B*.)

The rim of the tray is made by sewing with raffia or yarn over the coil of pine needles, cord, or reed. Pine needles or reed need to be soaked thoroughly in water for an hour before using.

Start sewing by laying the pine needles (or substitute) along one side of the double card. Put the sewing strand, threaded through the blunt needle, down through a hole (*C*). Sew down into the hole, out through bottom of cards, then over foundation coil, and into the next hole (as at arrow of second sketch). Stitch thus all around rim, once into each hole.

FANCY WING STITCH

To make the wing stitch on rim (*D*, page 146), take each stitch in second row down through the center of stitch just beneath it in the first row. The needle will pass through part of bundle of needles at this point. Continue with similar double stitches around the rows, forming radiating stitch lines. Make rim of tray three or four rows deep.

To finish off last row, take out part of pine needles (or whittle a solid rod) so there will be a gradual tapering down. Fasten last part of the coil with a double stitch, working the end back into the sewing.

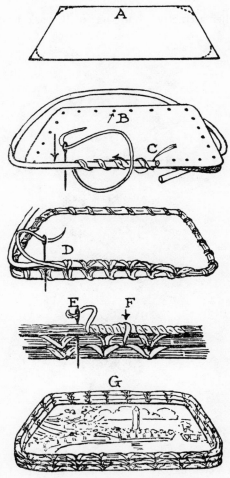

TRAY MADE FROM A POSTCARD

The entire last row may also be overcast (*E*), with **fastenings** down into next to the last row at intervals (*F*).

Shellac finished tray (*G*) when dry.

HANGING WALL BASKET OF LONG PINE NEEDLES WITH SHEATHS

To make the attractive hanging wall basket shown **below,**

A Hanging Wall Basket for Flowers, made of Long Pine
Needles with Sheaths and Cone for Decoration

gather a good number of long pine needles with their sheaths. Have ready some strong raffia or soft-toned woolen yarn for sewing and a large manilla cup or ice-cream carton to sew over. Make even clumps of the needles and sew them beneath their brackets or sheaths around the rim of the cup, using the raffia in over-and-over stitches. Reverse, to make the cross stitching. At the base of the basket, bind all the ends of the needles together with several rounds of the raffia. Fasten securely. Add a pine-tree cone for decoration.

For the handle, use two bunches of pine needles. Wind around each bunch with the raffia in cross stitching, as shown. Attach the ends of the clumps together to form the loop of the handle, overlapping them at least 3 inches. Attach the top or sheath ends of the clumps to the sides of the basket at the top, as shown. Insert a small glass into the carton to hold the flowers. Shellac the basket well to render durable.

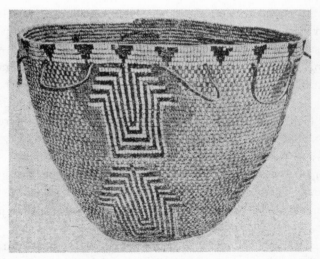

A BEAUTIFUL INDIAN CARRYING BASKET, MADE BY SEWING OVER
NATIVE GRASSES WITH SPLIT STITCH (PAGE 145)

CHAPTER 24

PLAITING BELTS AND BANDS

THERE ARE many interesting ways to make belts and bands (page 153) requiring very little equipment or expense. Craftsmen and hobbyists delight in making useful and inexpensive things for themselves. The process is so simple that often one end of the belt can be tied to a porch rail, bedpost, or nail on the wall, and the other to the chair in which you are sitting. That is your homemade loom.

PLAITED BELTS

All along the market places of southern countries, girls and women may be seen with a mere handful of yarns tied to a post or to the side of a building, making colorful things for themselves out of many materials. The gay bands they make develop rapidly into smart purses, scarves, and trimmings. These strips of belting require no buckles of wood or metal for fastening; tassels and braids, loops and ties of the belt yarn itself are more interesting and less expensive. Long yarn ends are finished into perky little pigtails; cut ends are braided and turned back into loops; huge tassels made of odds and ends of cut yarns are slipped through the loops and clasped around the belt to suit the individual waistline; small braids of the yarn may be quickly made into loops for jacket buttons, tassels for turbans, and other products.

Three or four colors are used for a belt, and a width of 1 inch to 3 inches is the most practical. Sew the plaited strips together in one of two ways—either with all colors going in the same direction,

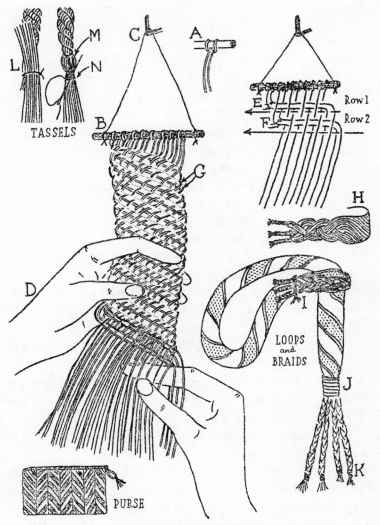

TASSELS

LOOPS
and
BRAIDS

PURSE

METHOD OF PLAITING BELTS

making continuous strips, or with adjacent stripes forming spear-heads, as in the purse shown above.

For materials, use tufting cotton or heavy strands of any kind, as well as heavy woolen yarns. Germantown or Peasant yarn or cotton of the same weight may be used satisfactorily, as may tufting cotton or doubled crochet yarn, in various colors.

PLAITING THE BELT (*page* 153)

To start a belt, cut strands double the desired length, with 1 inch added for shrinkage; fold each strand double; loop over a pencil or small round bar (*A*). Follow a stripe plan of your own creation, adding several dark strands, then some medium-colored strands and some light ones. Pull all ends even. Fasten a cord to ends of bar (*B*); slip this cord over a hook (*C*). Tie other end of belt to the post of a bed or the leg of a table; work with a fairly taut belt, sitting down at right or left of belt.

1st row. Hold strands with hands in position shown at *D*. With right forefinger, pass under and over each successive strand, as shown. The arrow marked Row 1 (sketch) takes the place of the finger in the sketch and represents the first row made. When the finger has gone all the way across, slip two left strands (see *E*) through opening or shed made; pass these through from left to right.

2nd row. Start again at farthest right; the forefinger passes *over* the strands it passed *under* before, and *under* those it passed *over* (see Row 2). When the finger has interlaced all across, bring two strands at extreme left (*F*) from left to right through the shed just made with the finger.

Alternate Rows 1 and 2. Strips of dark diagonal lines will show up against your lighter strands (*G*). After every row, carefully free the two strands, just brought through from left to right, from the other strands for about 2 feet along belt. After a time you will need to untie the knot at the unplaited end of the belt, and pull out all strands to make entirely free and to prevent clinging and possible tangling.

FINISHES FOR ENDS

Loops and Braids—To make a large, effective loop, braid ends into three large strands (*H*); fold back this thick braid and tie around main girdle with a narrow braid (*I*). Slip belt through. Make a collar around other end of belt (*J*). Group the yarn colors and braid into tight braids with tiny collars at ends (*K*).

Tassels—To make a large tassel to attach to an abrupt end of belt, cut six to ten strands of each color, measuring twice the length of tassel desired. Lay these cut strands flat along end of belt (*L*); tie tightly with strong cord. Now fold over the upper half of the strands, leave 1 inch for a tassel-head (*M*), and with a bright color wrap around tassel below *M* and insert needle up through collar thus made.

COLOR PLANS FOR BELTS

WIDE BELT WITH TASSELS

Cut strands 120 inches long; when folded they make 60 inches for plaiting. Cut 12 strands of each color.

Use four colors: color A, darkest (such as black); color B, dark (navy); color C, medium (red); color D, light (white).

Place on bar in following order: color A, four strands; color B, twelve strands; color C, twelve strands; color A, four strands; color D, twelve strands. Leave 8 inches unplaited before starting. Plait 44 inches. Leave 8 inches unplaited at end. Make a tassel at each end, adding eight strands of each color.

NARROW BELT

Cut strands 120 inches long; when folded they make 60 inches for plaiting.

Use four colors: color A, accent color (such as very dark brown), eight strands; color B, dark color (henna), six strands; color C, medium (yellow), six strands; color D, light (ivory), six strands.

Place on bar in following order: color B, six strands; color A, two strands; color C, six strands; color A, two strands; color D, six strands. When belt is finished, add braids or tassels.

ANOTHER NARROW BELT

Cut strands 120 inches long.

Use three colors: color A, dark (blue), eight strands; color B, medium (red), ten strands; color C, light (white), ten strands.

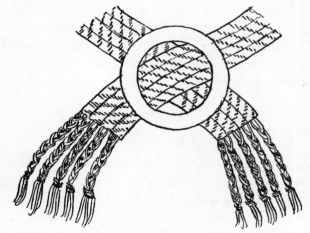

ATTRACTIVE ACCESSORIES MADE OF NARROW WOVEN BANDS
(See also opposite page)

Fold double and place on bar in following order: color A, four strands; color B, ten strands; color A, four strands; color C, ten strands.

Other color combinations may be worked out.

BRAIDED PURSE (*pages* 153 *and* 157)

For a purse, use any of the given belt designs. Cut short strips 8½ inches long. Sew together enough strips to make a piece 8½ by 11 inches. Fold double into size 8½ by 5½ inches. If using narrow 1½-inch belts, you will need 72 inches of belting, 1½ inches wide. If using a belt about 3 inches wide, 36 inches of finished belting will be needed.

First make lining of buckram covered with satin, measuring when finished 5 by 8 inches. Fold purse material into a piece 5½ by 8½ inches and overcast at two side edges; press down top edge, which will hold zipper. Slip in lining and baste. Attach zipper between lining and purse. Blindstitch beneath lining.

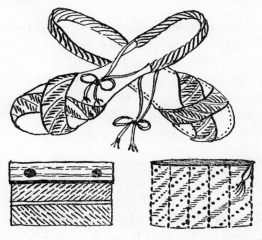

BRAIDED SANDALS (*above*)

Use any of the methods given for making narrow bands. Attach to quilted or felt slipper soles. Make narrow bands for heels of sandals and wider bands to cover instep. Attach handmade cord ties and tassels to insteps.

CHAPTER 25

WEAVING WITH SMALL APPLIANCES

I N THE home, narrow strips make successful tie-backs for curtains, strips to wrap around stored linen, or gay bookmarks for
treasured volumes. The usefulness of these strips is equaled
only by the fascination of putting together bright colors and watch-
ing them grow into the colorful fabric. The weaving may be done
out-of-doors or on a porch; the equipment is so light in weight
that it can be taken anywhere.

MAKING A HEDDLE FRAME (page 160)

The weaving of a narrow band is both constructive and enjoy-
able. Only thirteen strands of yarn are used to make the body or
warp of the band illustrated. For this work you can make the
lightweight weaving frame at home at practically no cost, for the
wood is taken from a cigar box. The little handmade frame is
called a heddle frame.

MATERIALS

A shallow wooden cigar box measuring about 6 by 8 by
$2\frac{1}{2}$ inches.

A coping saw; a file; a hammer; $\frac{1}{2}$-inch brads (the brads from
the box may be used); pencil and ruler.

CONSTRUCTION

To make a heddle frame (page 160), carefully separate the sides
of the box from the base. Use the two end pieces (*A*), measuring

2¼ by 6 inches, and trim off one of the long side pieces to make a third piece the same size (*B*). Divide all three pieces into four even strips (*C*) and saw them apart with a fine saw. You will now have twelve strips 6 inches long and ½ inch wide. Save two of these strips for braces at top and bottom of frame. At the center of each of the other ten strips bore a hole ⅛ inch in diameter (*D*), using an awl or a red-hot nail held carefully between pincers. You will discover that these holes are to serve as eyes for the warp thread to pass through.

To put these pieces together to make the frame, mark off on the two pieces that you have saved for top and bottom, spaces for ½-inch strips with ⅛ inch between them (*E*). Sandpaper the ½-inch strips down to a little less than ½ inch; it will now be possible to put the ten strips along the 6-inch strip at top and bottom. Tack down the ten strips with ½-inch brads against the top and bottom pieces (*F*). To strengthen, saw out two extra strips (*F*) to place against the front at top and bottom, thus enclosing the vertical strips between back and front supports. The frame is now ready for threading and weaving.

THREADING THE FRAME TO WEAVE STRIPS

To try out your frame, weave a narrow strip about 1 inch wide, like one of the narrow strips used for the jacket at *P*. For this you need only thirteen strands of thread. The full width of the heddle frame will accommodate nineteen strands, ten through the holes and nine through the spaces, weaving a band about 2 inches wide. To make a belt 2 inches wide, add double threads for edges at the very outside of the frame (*G*). But use only thirteen threads for the 1-inch strip. Find the center space (arrow) and count to each side—first sending a thread through a hole, then through a space, then through a hole, space, and so on—until you have threaded all thirteen threads alternately through the holes and spaces (finishing at arrows, *H*).

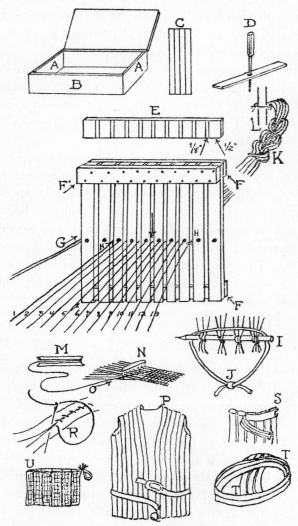

WOODEN HEDDLE MADE FROM A BOX AND ARTICLES MADE
FROM FINISHED STRIPS

ARRANGEMENT OF THREADS FOR VARIEGATED BAND

For a woven strip, prepare the strands 3 yards long, using heavy cotton or Germantown yarn, or odds and ends of thread used double to make a smaller strand. For a cotton warp you may use 6-strand perle floss most effectively, and the cotton weaves up easily. Across this, perle or wool weft may be woven, so that the result is a heavy, good-looking belt.

Prepare the thirteen strands as follows: one black, one orange, one green, two tan, one white, one black (center), one white, two tan, one green, one orange, one black. Thread in the order given, starting at center space with black, then white through the hole, tan through the slot, tan through the hole, and so on, on each side of the center. Pull all the threads through the heddle, make their ends even, and tie them in groups of three or four to a crossbar of wood or a pencil 6 inches long (*I*). Slip a noose of strong cord over the bar (*J*) and attach this noose temporarily to a post or hook. The noose is to be attached to your belt later, when weaving.

From the other side of the heddle frame, clasp the group of threads in the palm of your left hand; with the right hand remove with a comb any tangles of the warp. Keep moving along the warp until you are at the end away from the crossbar. When all the threads have been untangled and are at the same tension, start making a chain about 1 yard from the other end (*K*). With heavy twine fasten this other end of the chain to a post, such as a bedpost or a tree trunk (*L*, page 160; see also page 162).

The weaving is done by lifting the frame up and down and running a cross-thread, or weft, back and forth through the opening, or shed, just made. To hold the weft-thread, make a weaving stick or shuttle 6 inches long and 1 inch wide, from the fourth side of the cigar box (*M*). Cut out ends to make them concave, and sandpaper smooth. Wind shuttle with white perle floss. This adds luster and lessens the weight of the finished band. For a warm wool band, weave with a soft zephyr yarn.

WEAVING WITH THE HEDDLE FRAME

Before starting to weave, slip the noose of the pencil-bar about your waist, or attach it to your belt. Push back your chair until warp is taut. Push frame down with left hand; put shuttle through opening, or shed, and leave a row of thread; push this row up close to the crossbar with a comb (N). Now change hands and lift frame up with right hand, inserting weft from left side (as shown

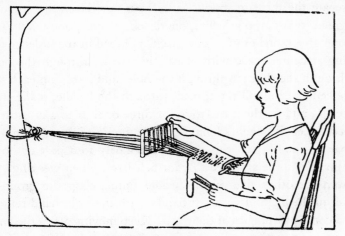

WEAVING WITH A WOODEN HEDDLE

above). When you have left the second row of weft-thread, push it against first row with comb. So that there will not be a loose starting thread hanging, insert the end of the thread back into this second row and pack with comb. It will not show.

For third row, lower frame with left hand; for fourth row raise frame with right. Continue, and each time pass shuttle through the shed, weaving a row of weft-thread. In a short time these three motions—making the shed, putting through the thread, and packing it close with a comb—will become so automatic that they will follow one another rapidly. After a little practice you may discard the comb, using the flat side of the shuttle to press the last row up tightly *after* the new shed is made. As the warp is gradually used up, loosen the chain (*K*) and allow to come forward to complete your project.

Keeping a Good Selvage

There is a little trick about laying in the weft-threads which keeps the selvage, or edge, even. Lay in each thread across the warp diagonally (see *O*, page 160). Keep comb parallel to last row of material; push with it against the diagonal thread until it comes up against the other. The additional thread used to make the slanting line instead of a straight crossline will be evenly distributed or taken up by the warp without pulling in the edge of the material.

MAKING ARTICLES FROM FINISHED STRIPS

Making a Jacket (*page* 160)

First cut out a pattern from unbleached muslin in vertical jacket style to fit yourself. As you finish a strip of weaving, cut it into lengths to fit your pattern from shoulder seam to base (page 160, *P* to *Q*). Pin each strip to the muslin pattern. Proceed all around the jacket in this way. The strips under the arms will be shorter, of course. Allow 1 inch for shrinkage of all strips. When the entire muslin pattern is covered, start sewing strips together with the same 6-strand floss as that of the weft, or with the wool you have used (page 160, Sketch *R*). When seams are together, remove muslin. Sew front and back panels together to make shoulder seams, and face with binding. Turn down all cut edges $\frac{1}{2}$ inch, and face with binding (*S*).

Making Hat and Purse (*page* 160)

For beret, use three strips 11 inches long to make each section across top (page 160, *T*). For the headband, use two strips sewed together. The parts of the beret may be carefully pinned together to fit the head, then sewed by hand with the soft weft-floss.

For the purse (*U*), use six strips 8 inches long, seamed together and folded in the envelope shape shown. The size when finished will be about 4 by 6 inches. Line and insert a 5-inch zipper.

Hats and purses of a variety of shapes may be made. Patterns may be purchased and covered with the strips of material as described.

Ten More Uses for Handwoven Strips (*page 165*)

1. The bag at 1 measures 10 inches in length and 6 inches in depth. For the handles use a strip of material folded double lengthwise, padding it with cotton to give it body. The bag may be lined and a zipper added if desired.

2. A strip of belt material 6 to 8 inches long fringed at the ends makes an effective bookmark.

3. To make a luncheon set of doilies on your heddle frame, thread with light colors for eight strips, and use a dark strip to cut and divide into borders. Simply sew the pieces together in any way you choose. Hand-stitch across the ends, and fringe.

4. This design is for a doily with strips running crosswise.

5. Woven strips may be joined with heavy crochet stitches to make the bag shown at 5.

6. By sewing a long strip round and round a cylindrical form like a carton, an attractive container may be devised.

7. For a pincushion, take the top of a round carton, turn upside down, stuff with sawdust, cover with a piece of printed material, and run the handwoven strip around the edge as shown. This trimming gives body and color.

8. Handwoven strips make effective bands to snap around sets of towels or linen doilies. Line the strip with one of the colors, making a point at one end. Attach snaps.

9. For a gay touch in the clubroom or kitchen, make a memorandum pad by putting a strap of the woven material around cardboard covered with wallpaper. Slip the note pad over the strap as

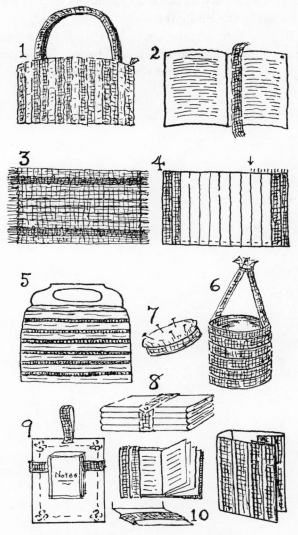

USES FOR STRIPS WOVEN ON THE HEDDLE

shown. A handle may be made by running a loop of the material through a slit in the cardboard.

10. Book covers may be made by sewing strips together and pasting down over cardboard fronts and backs. Single strips looped make good pockets to slip over the back of a folio.

CHAPTER 26

WRAPPING AND WINDING PROJECTS

PICTURE FRAME OF CARDBOARD AND RAFFIA
(page 168)

A SMALL PICTURE frame can be made by wrapping raffia round and round a piece of cardboard that has been cut in a chosen shape. By using two colors of raffia you can make a stripe design along the frame edge. Two frames may be sewed together to make a double standing picture frame. Germantown yarn in bright colors may be used in place of the raffia.

MATERIALS

For one frame, use two pieces of cardboard cut from a box or the back of a pad, two colors of raffia or yarn, a sharp knife for scoring, sharp scissors, library paste, and a steel-edged ruler.

MAKING FRONT AND BACK OF FRAME

Analyze sketches on page 168. Then cut a piece of cardboard 4 by 5 inches. Draw opening at center $\frac{5}{8}$ inch in from edge all around. Cut this hole by scoring with sharp knife against steel edge of ruler. Sandpaper edges.

To wrap the front, plan design by marking places all along edge for color accents (*B*). Clip off corners $\frac{1}{8}$ inch (*C*). Start wrapping near corner with the lighter of your two colors (*D*). Cover the end of the yarn with the wrapping as shown. At the corner introduce

the dark strand and wrap at right angles, stitch 1 ; then wrap
around opposite side at right angles, stitch 2. Pass once again

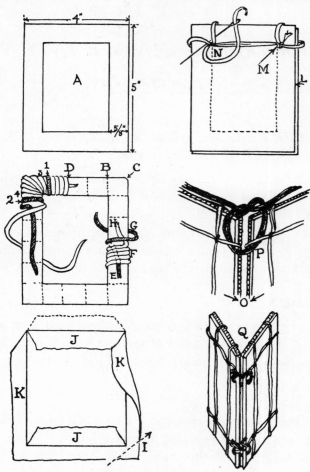

PICTURE FRAME OF CARDBOARD AND RAFFIA

around stitch 1 and stitch 2 to make them strong. Now hold the
dark strand tightly in your left hand. Pick up light strand with
right hand and fill in corner as shown, using stitch 3, then 4, and

so on. The heavy, dark stitches keep the longer corner stitches from slipping. Apply a little glue at tip of corner if necessary.

To introduce a dark color or to add a new strand, place new strand *E* (page 168) under regular strand *F*. Cover the new strand with several wrappings, then bring it out (as at *G*), and put the old strand under it (as at *H*). From now on, wrap over the old strand with the new one. Wrap entire rim of frame by alternating colors of raffia in this way.

For back of frame, cut cardboard $3\frac{3}{4}$ by $4\frac{3}{4}$ inches. Cut this slightly smaller than the front, so that the back will not show when attached to the front. Cover the back with paper the color of the raffia wrappings. Cut the paper $\frac{1}{2}$ inch larger than back, all around. Cut paper off across corners (*I*), leaving just $\frac{1}{16}$ inch beyond corner. Paste down two ends (*J*), then two sides (*K*).

To conceal the turned-over edges, cut another piece of paper $3\frac{1}{2}$ by $4\frac{1}{2}$ inches. Paste this down over entire back. Place back under a weight to dry for several hours and to make it flat.

Attaching Back to Front of Frame

You have now finished making the wrapped front part of the single frame, and the back part is covered with paper. Next, these two parts must be bound together neatly.

Lay back against front (*L*). In this sketch the back part is shown, and the opening of the front is indicated by dotted lines. Thread a long strand of raffia or yarn through a sharp, strong darning needle. Start at a corner (*M*), using raffia the color of the stripes. Put needle down through corner of opening, then around one side and out through hole. Now wrap raffia at right angles around other side and come out through same hole again. Fasten raffia or yarn in a knot. This knot finishes fastening at one corner. The strand goes entirely around both back and front in making the tie.

Proceed to next corner (*N*) and repeat same stitches as for first corner. Then pass to third corner and to fourth. After fourth corner is fastened, carry the strand up to the first corner and tie its end to first knot (*M*).

DOUBLE PICTURE FRAME

Place together the two back edges of two complete frames (page 168, at *O*). With a strong piece of raffia or yarn used double, tie a knot around raffia strands that were used at corners and are now opposite each other in the two frames (*P*). Make a loop or knot about ½ inch along to insure leeway for opening and closing of frame. Make an attachment at both top and bottom. The finished frame is shown at *Q*.

To render frame durable, give it a coat of shellac on back and front. Slip a piece of cardboard into opening between back and front, where picture is to be inserted, to keep any shellac from sticking at this point. When entire frame is dry, insert pictures and place frame open on your stand. For small frames of this type, glass is not necessary; the pictures may be covered with a sheet of cellophane.

WOVEN BOOK ENDS (*page* 171)

These book ends woven over wooden blocks will suggest other projects to the craftsman. The shape, size, and color of the book ends will depend upon their relation to furniture, rugs, and wallpaper.

MATERIALS

Spokes—Cut fourteen lengths of round reed or reed substitute 11 inches long.

Weavers—Six full-length pieces of flat winding reed or flat fiber reed.

Tacks—Twenty-eight small carpet tacks for tacking on spokes.

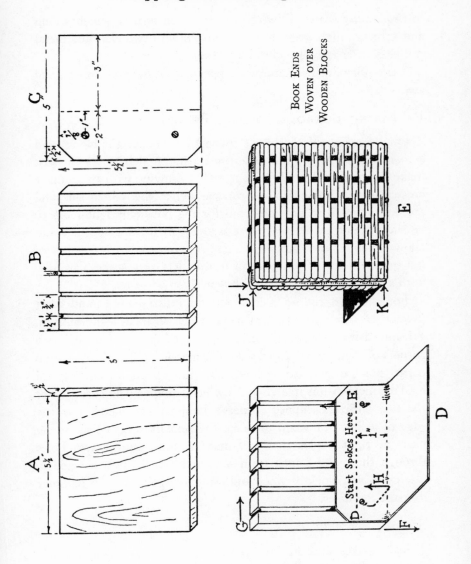

BOOK ENDS
WOVEN OVER
WOODEN BLOCKS

Boards and braces—Two pieces of ½-inch board 5½ inches long and 5 inches high (page 171, Sketch *A*). Cut two pieces of metal 5 inches wide and 5½ inches long (Sketch *C*).

Tools—Saw, plane, hammer, nippers, sheet metal, snippers, and awl.

Preparing Boards and End Braces

On the wide side (5 by 5½ inches) of the upright block, and across the narrow top and base (measuring ½ inch by 5½ inches), make six grooves (Sketch *B*, page 171) by sawing with an ordinary crosscut saw. These grooves run parallel to the 5-inch side and are deep enough to provide room for the No. 3 upright reeds to be laid through them. Start first groove ½ inch from side edge and allow ⅛ inch for each groove, making six grooves ¾ inch apart, with last groove ½ inch from edge of board. Measure spaces carefully with a ruler, and draw lines with pencil for saw-cuts.

For the two right-angled braces to make books stand erect (Sketch *C*), use two pieces of metal 5 by 5½ inches—aluminum, galvanized-iron sheeting, zinc, copper, or brass. Cut off two corners of each metal piece as shown, measuring ½ inch from each corner point to get cutting line. Use tin snippers for cutting and hold the metal firmly in a vise. Now bend down a 2-inch section of the side with the clipped corners; hammer the metal over the edge of a block of wood to make the remaining 3 inches of the piece at right angles to the 2-inch section. Punch two holes through the metal ⅞ inch from sides and 1 inch from bent edge, placing it on a block of wood and using a large nail and a hammer to make the holes.

Steps in Weaving

Soak spokes and flat weavers in tepid water about twenty minutes. Place the six No. 3 reed spokes into the sawed-out grooves; tack the end of each, 1 inch above the base on inner side of book end (see page 171, Sketch *D*, dotted line *D–E*). Carry each spoke up following the groove to other side, down again as far as base, but not under it. Tack spokes close to base, and allow remaining ends of spokes to extend straight down 1½ inches below block while proceeding (Sketch *D*, arrow *F*).

Start to weave by inserting a flat weaver under first spoke at upper left corner (arrow *G*, Sketch *D*). Carefully tack down its end flush with edge. Interlace the weaver from left to right, passing under and over the spokes. Draw weaver to opposite corner, turn around board snugly, return on other side, continuing with the Under-and-Over Weave. Draw every row up tightly and close to last row of weaving. To add a new flat weaver, lay new strand against old weaver behind the last spoke covered.

When you have woven continuously around book end to within 2 inches of base, tack metal in position on inner side of book end, against the starting ends of the spokes. From now on, the weaving strand must pass completely across the metal on this side, while it continues to pass under and over the spokes on the outer or front side. When you have woven with firm, closely packed stitches as far as base, cut off the weaver, allowing 2 inches extra, and tuck this end up under the weaving.

Now soak the 1½ inches of remaining spoke-ends hanging down on outer side. Squeeze with pincers or nip slightly, so that ends will bend readily up under block of wood. Bend them close into grooves under block, sharpen their ends, and tuck them up into the remaining 1 inch of empty groove left by the starting ends (see Sketch *D*, arrow below line *D–E*, at *H*).

To decorate sides, cut two pieces of the ½-inch flat reed. Tack this on each book end around the two sides and top (as at *J*, Sketch *E*). Tack ends flush against base of block, but not under it (Sketch *E*, point *K*).

STAINING OR PAINTING

Color your book ends to harmonize with the room. The colors most suitable for living rooms are bronze, gold or silver, or soft tones of rose, taupe, green, or brown. Use stain or paint. When book ends are thoroughly dry, cut two pieces of heavy felt or blotting paper 3 by 5½ inches. Paste this under the metal bases of the book ends. Use metal glue or cement or airplane glue.

Other types of book ends may be worked out. You might try a pattern with gable ends, with the reed woven around a 4-inch base and rising upward from the sides. The gable can be made of board with the uprights placed over its edges. In finishing, the gable may be stained one color and the base another color.

The making and marketing of these book ends will be profitable. Make them up in quantities, and place them in gift shops or novelty stores. If artistically planned and well made, they should bring a dollar and a half or two dollars a pair.

CHAPTER 27

MATS OF CORD AND TWINE

Hot-plate mats made of cord are never out of style. Doormats are made in the same way but of a stronger cord. Both mats are so simply woven that a child could make them. And as the frames can be constructed out of four pieces of wood, the only material you need to buy is the cord itself. These mats wear indefinitely. The table mats wash well in warm soapsuds. After they have dried you can restore the original fluffiness of the fringe by combing it.

MATERIALS AND EQUIPMENT

For a set of hot-plate mats: Frame made from two pieces of wood $\frac{3}{8}$ by $\frac{5}{8}$ by 13 inches, and two pieces of wood $\frac{3}{8}$ by $\frac{5}{8}$ by 11 inches; one ball of mercerized cotton for each mat.

For the doormat: Frame made from two pieces of wood $\frac{1}{2}$ by $1\frac{1}{2}$ by 32 inches, and two pieces of wood $\frac{1}{2}$ by $1\frac{1}{2}$ by 24 inches; several balls of twine, hemp, or juteen, depending upon the size of the ball.

MAKING THE HOT-PLATE FRAME (*page* 176)

The simplest frame for hot-plate mats is made from four pieces of wood with nail pegs (as shown on page 176, *R*). The two long bars are $\frac{5}{8}$ inch wide and 13 inches long but only $\frac{3}{8}$ inch thick. The two short bars are $\frac{5}{8}$ by 11 inches and $\frac{3}{8}$ inch thick. Nail the bars together $\frac{1}{2}$ inch from the corners, with the two long bars on top. Between these long bars insert two additional short bars (*S*), making the level of all bars the same. These bars are $\frac{5}{8}$ inch wide

and ⅜ inch thick and fit snugly between the long bars. The nails
are then spaced ½ inch apart and hammered along the sides as
illustrated. The thread is wound around the nails (as shown
below).

If you want to make a more substantial frame, follow these
directions (illustrated below at *A–G*):

Use four bars of wood. The two long bars measure ⅝ by
13 inches and are ⅜ inch thick. The two short bars measure ⅝ by
11 inches and are ⅜ inch thick. In the drawing (below) the long
bar is marked *A*, the short one marked *B*. Measure ½ inch from
the ends of all four bars and, by sawing halfway into the wood and
cutting out the wood with a knife or chisel, make the cut-outs
marked *C*. These cut-outs are 11⁄16 inch wide, or a little wider than

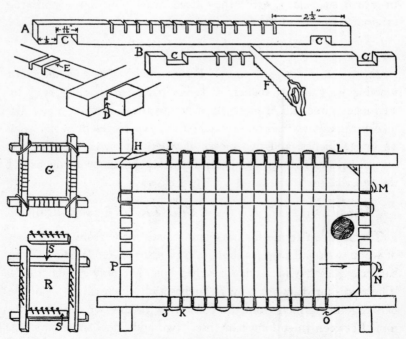

CONSTRUCTION OF WOODEN FRAME FOR WEAVING MATS

the bars, which are ⅝ inch. They allow the bars to be locked together (*D*). The notches (*E*) begin 2½ inches from the ends of the bars and should be ½ inch apart. They are made by sawing halfway down into the wood (*F*). Notice that the long bars (*A*) have these saw-cuts made on the opposite side from the larger cuts (*C*), while the shorter bars (*B*) have the saw-cuts on the same side as the *C* cuts. Lock the four corners (shown at *G*) and tie them firmly together with a string.

WEAVING THE HOT-PLATE MATS (*page* 176, H–P)

To weave the table mats use soft mercerized cotton floss or plain washcloth cotton about the size of ordinary white cord. The floss is preferable for gift mats. Tie one end securely around one corner of the frame (page 176, *H*) and carry the floss to the nearest notch or nail on the upper side (marked *I*). Loop it around the notch or nail and carry across to the opposite one (*J*). Carry through this, then to *K*, continuing back and forth until you reach the corner (*L*). Do not pull the thread too tightly, but make it tight enough to lie straight and firm.

At *L*, carry the thread under the corner of frame to the first notch or nail on the short side (*M*). Then go back and forth as indicated until corner (*N*) is reached. Now start weaving vertically again, on top of the threads already laid (shown by arrow at *O*). When you reach the last corner (*J*), go to *P* and weave horizontally again. Continue weaving alternately vertically and horizontally until the mat is about ¼ inch thick when squeezed together with the fingers. Tie the last thread to a corner. You are now ready to tie the squares.

TYING MATS INTO SQUARE CROSSES
(*page* 178, A–D)

For tying you may use a contrasting color of floss of the same thickness as that used for the rest of the mat. Thread a blunt darning needle with the floss or cotton, the end of which is tied around the intersecting threads at one corner (below, *A–C*). Now make a tie at each intersection of the threads, going diagonally

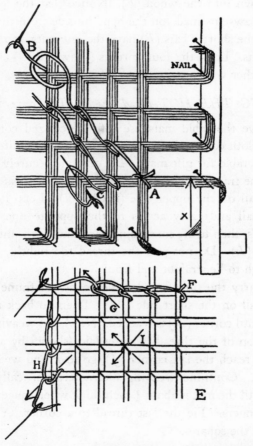

TYING WOVEN MATS INTO SQUARE CROSSES. (See also opposite page.)

across toward the opposite corner. This tie is nothing more than a buttonhole stitch with the thread passing completely under the crossing threads (*B*). If the mat is square you will finish at the opposite corner; if it is oblong, you will finish somewhere on the side. In either case, pass the needle to the next diagonal row (*C*) and go across again. Continue back and forth diagonally until you

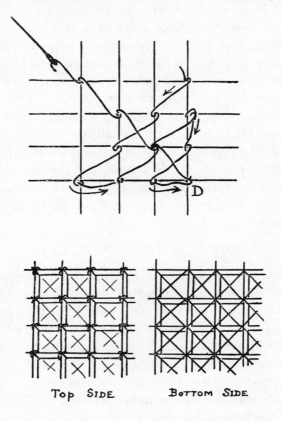

Top Side   Bottom Side

have tied each intersection of threads once. Now take the opposite diagonal (*D*) and make the same kind of buttonhole ties over the entire mat surface. You have now bound each intersection twice, so that each one seems to be caught with a cross-stitch. Now cut out the mat, cutting close to the side bars (shown by arrow at *X*). The untied side is used as the top or right side.

To weave a square mat on an oblong frame, simply stop weaving on the long side as soon as desired length is reached, and carry the thread over to the short side directly, continuing the horizontal weaving. You can also weave square mats on the adjustable frames, to be described shortly under "Circular Mats."

There is another method of tying up the squares. This method is shown on page 178, at *E*. The same knot is used, but you take a horizontal and vertical direction, tying along on top of the rows of weaving threads. Beginning at one corner (*F*), proceed to the opposite corner, keeping the needle slanting up in direction shown at arrow, *G*. Go back and forth over all the horizontal rows, then knot all along the vertical rows (*H*). These knots will lie on top of those already made. While knotting the vertical rows, be sure to have the needle point (as at arrow, *H*) just at right angles to the direction (*G*), so that each corner will be clasped in four places (see *I*, arrows).

COLOR SCHEME FOR MATS

Hot-plate mats in two-color combinations are attractive. To make a set in yellow and white, start weaving back and forth with yellow, and continue until you have made a complete round. Tie with white, and the appearance will be that of mottled white and yellow. Any pastel shade may be combined with white. Use colors that match your china.

A set of mats may be composed of one square or one large oblong made on the full size of the frame, and two smaller oblongs or squares made by omitting two or three of the notches or nails on both the long and short sides.

OVAL MATS (*page* 181, *A–C*)

Oval mats are made on the same rectangular frames, and the cord is wound on the frame exactly as it is for oblong mats. Tying up the squares is different, however. (See page 181.) The three

crossings at each corner are not tied at all. You begin at *B* and tie
in the direction of the arrow (to *C*). Now keep on tying diagonally
back and forth until the mat is all tied. The same stitch is used
and the method is the same as already described, except that the

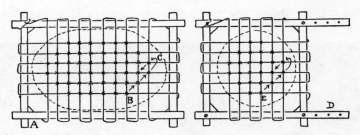

METHODS OF WEAVING OVAL OR ROUND MATS

three corner crossings are left untied. In cutting the mat from the
frame cut close to the sides. When the mat has been removed from
the frame, trim it to an oval form (see dotted lines).

CIRCULAR MATS (*above*, D–E)

A circular mat is made on either a square or an oblong adjustable
frame (shown above). You can make an adjustable frame out
of the frame made with nails (see *R*, page 176). Simply use
screws instead of nails, and bore holes for the screws at different
distances along the long sides (*above*, *D*). By sliding the short
side and adjusting the screws, you can make a mat of any size on
this single frame. In the chart it is adjusted for a square or circular
mat.

Wind around mat as you would a square mat. The method of
winding never varies for any shape mat. After you have finished
weaving, begin tying (*above*, at *E*), again omitting the three
crossings at each corner. Tie diagonally by the buttonhole stitch
described. After cutting the mat, trim in circular form, as shown
by the dotted lines.

DOORMATS

Weave a doormat just as you would a hot-plate mat, but use twine, jute, juteen, or hemp. The frames may be any size. For a doormat that measures 19 by 27 inches, the frame required has two long bars $1\frac{1}{2}$ inches wide, 32 inches long, and $\frac{1}{2}$ inch thick;

A USEFUL HANDMADE DOORMAT

and two short bars $1\frac{1}{2}$ inches wide, 24 inches long, and $\frac{1}{2}$ inch thick. A doormat frame is easily made by the nail method (page 176, *R*). The nails used along the bars are 2 inches long, spaced 1 inch apart. A doormat is tied in the horizontal and vertical way (page 178, *E*). A doormat will give years of service, and should sell for a good price.

PART IV

Weaving Chair Seats

CHAPTER 28

CHAIR CANING

T HE CANING and recaning of chair seats has been for genera-
tions a practical craft. Almost every home has some piece
of furniture in need of recaning. Aside from being of
economic value, this project is helpful training for the craftsman.

CHAIR CANE AND OTHER SEATING MATERIALS

Chair-seating materials are generally classified as follows:

Fine fine cane   Oval reed for porch chairs
Fine cane   Hickory splints
Medium cane   Birch splints
Common cane   Genuine rush
Binding cane   Imitation rush
                        Reed splints

The tools required are nose pliers, diagonal cutters, sandpaper,
nippers, and an awl.

METHOD OF CANING (*page* 186 *to* 188)

If the project is the recaning of a seat, first remove the old cane.
Clean and thoroughly sandpaper all rough surfaces. Remove cane
from all holes and clean holes carefully. Pull six canes from the
loop-end of the bundle and soak in a tub of water for a few hours.
The soaking not only makes the cane more manageable but aids
the shrinking, pulling the seat taut.

Layer 1 (shown in diagram below). Start one end of first cane down through the hole (*A*); then bring it up through corner hole to fasten the end. Take the other end of the cane and begin

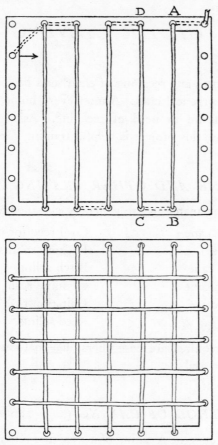

CANING CHAIR SEATS: FIRST AND SECOND LAYERS

the weaving of the cane seat by passing it across the seat to the first hole on opposite side (*B*). Put it through this hole from the top down, plugging it in, then up through the next hole (*C*) and across to the second hole on opposite side (*D*).

Continue crossing from side to side until every opposite pair of holes is joined by a firmly drawn cane. If you run out of cane and must start a new piece, plug the old end into a hole and start the

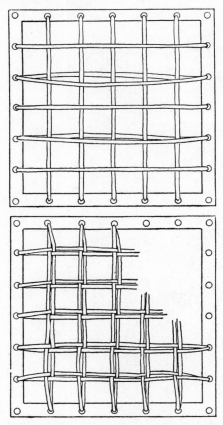

CANING CHAIR SEATS: THIRD AND FOURTH LAYERS

new end in same hole under the same plug. A knot may be tied at the end of the new cane and drawn up through a hole, the knot remaining fastened just below the hole.

Layer 2 (page 186). When the seat has been covered with the first layer of cane, run a second layer in opposite direction between the holes until every pair of holes has been joined. The canes must always be kept right side up with the smooth, rounded surface on top. The seat, when woven with the two sets of canes from

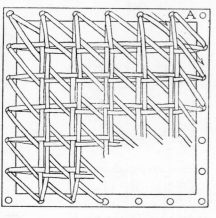

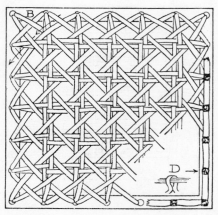

CANING CHAIR SEATS: FIFTH AND SIXTH LAYERS

front to back and from side to side, will present a checkered appearance.

Layer 3 (page 187). Weave third layer directly above first layer and through the same holes in the same way.

Layer 4 (page 187). Shove strands of third layer to the left while putting in fourth layer which you weave by interlacing strand under and over the strands of the first and third layers.

Layer 5 (page 188). Start the cane weaver from the corner *A* of the chair seat (analyze sketch) and weave diagonally across the seat to the hole opposite. Weave under two vertical canes, then over two horizontal canes (arrows in sketch), and continue until you have woven the fifth layer of cane diagonally across between the former layers. For fifth and sixth layers the weaving will be simplified if you can find an old piece of chair caning and trace the stitches carefully.

Layer 6 (page 188). Complete the seat by connecting holes diagonally in opposite direction. Start at corner *B* as shown in sketch for sixth layer, and carry weaver over two vertical strands and under two horizontal strands (as at arrows).

Binding the Seat. Take a large half-round cane and lay it flat over the holes around the chair seat. Use a smaller reed to bind, as follows: Thread the small reed up through each hole, passing over the binding cane and going down into the same hole again, as sketched at *D*, Layer 6. Draw reed tightly and plug in the beginning and ending holes, so as to grip and hold the ends firmly in place.

STAINING AND FINISHING

The method of staining and finishing cane seats usually depends upon the condition of the cane and the kind of furniture. Often a single coat of shellac provides enough finish for a cane seat.

CHAPTER 29

WEAVING RUSH AND TWINE SEATS

THERE IS a charm and dignity to the old-fashioned rush-seated chairs that will never be supplanted by newer models. If you are lucky enough to own a few, never discard them. Antique dealers are paying big sums for them, while factories today are manufacturing imitations of these chairs. Perhaps you have some in your attic—with the seats out and the paint or varnish almost gone. With a little work you can make distinctive chairs out of these discards. First they must be reseated. And the directions are simple if followed step by step.

Rush-seated chairs were made of the rush fibers that were once plentiful. Nowadays rush is difficult to obtain and prepare, and raffia is used as a substitute. Raffia is really desirable for chair bottoms, for it is easy to procure and pleasant to use and may be dyed any color to match the wood of the chair.

A single strand of raffia is not as strong as a strand of rush, but if three or four raffia strands are twisted together they will be as tough as one of rush. Simply twist the raffia as you proceed with the chair bottom, adding new strands when the old ones end. The raffia rope that you are making will be as strong as a clothesline, and the many ropes put together in the chair bottom will make a firm base. Rush or imitation rush may of course be used.

If your chair is to be painted, use a color of raffia that blends. The seat will be much softer in appearance than if painted with oil colors when finished. Unlike reed, raffia should not be kept wet.

Instead, each piece is run through a moist sponge just before using. To prevent drying, it is well to keep the raffia in a damp cloth inside a box.

The seat is made by twisting the strands into a cord and winding this cord around the chair rails. The four upper horizontal rails

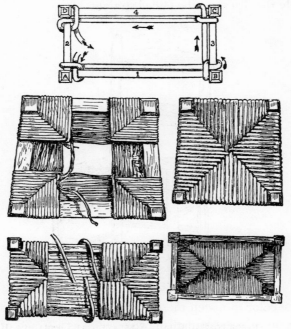

RESEATING A RUSH-BOTTOMED CHAIR

are the only ones that we wind (above—1, 2, 3, 4). The cord is first tied to the left handrail, then wound around the front rail, and then back to the left one again. Next it crosses to the right rail and returns to the front one; then it crosses to the back and returns to the right rail; finally it crosses to the left, returns, and goes around the back rail. It keeps twisting around in a figure eight. A square seat finishes at the center; but an oblong seat requires winding in and out of the space across the middle. See corners *A*, *B*, *C*, and *D*.

To twist the raffia into a cord, take the strands between the thumb and forefinger of the right hand, about a foot away from the tie at the beginning, and roll them into a tight, smooth, cord. When the cord is about $\frac{1}{8}$ inch wide, $1\frac{1}{2}$ feet long, and begins to curl up, it is ready to wind around the rails. Do not twist the cord so tightly that it cannot be pulled straight.

A RUSH-BOTTOMED CHAIR, RESEATED AS DESCRIBED HERE

If you have neither the time nor the patience for the slow process of making raffia rope, a seat may be woven with a ball of twine. The twine should be $\frac{1}{8}$ inch thick, of good strength, and of light color. The twine is wound about the chair rails as the raffia was. Linen twine, the strong ropy kind, is the best for this purpose. This seat can be woven quickly and with pleasing results.

REFINISHING CHAIRS

After an old chair is reseated, it usually needs to be repainted or revarnished to make it entirely fresh. You may have this done professionally, but it is surprisingly simple to refinish old chairs yourself. First, all the old paint and varnish must be taken off with paint remover. When the varnish is entirely washed off and the wood is thoroughly dry, the chair should be painted and allowed to dry again. Now varnish it to a glossy finish. If you prefer a dull finish, varnish may be applied several times, then rubbed down with powdered pumice between coats. The only tools required for dull finishing are oo sandpaper to smooth the work at the beginning, and some soft cloths with a little boiled oil to wipe the surface afterwards. The pumice should be applied only with a cloth dipped in oil, to avoid scratching the finish. The cost of paint remover, sandpaper, pumice stone, varnish, and paint is less than the cost of having one chair reseated, and there will be enough material to refinish half a dozen. Whenever your furniture is injured, this equipment will make it good as new.

INDEX

A CATALOGUE OF SELECTED DOVER BOOKS
IN ALL FIELDS OF INTEREST

A CATALOGUE OF SELECTED DOVER
BOOKS IN ALL FIELDS OF INTEREST

CONDITIONED REFLEXES, Ivan P. Pavlov. Full translation of most complete statement of Pavlov's work; cerebral damage, conditioned reflex, experiments with dogs, sleep, similar topics of great importance. 430pp. 5⅜ x 8½. 60614-7 Pa. $4.50

NOTES ON NURSING: WHAT IT IS, AND WHAT IT IS NOT, Florence Nightingale. Outspoken writings by founder of modern nursing. When first published (1860) it played an important role in much needed revolution in nursing. Still stimulating. 140pp. 5⅜ x 8½. 22340-X Pa. $2.50

HARTER'S PICTURE ARCHIVE FOR COLLAGE AND ILLUSTRATION, Jim Harter. Over 300 authentic, rare 19th-century engravings selected by noted collagist for artists, designers, decoupeurs, etc. Machines, people, animals, etc., printed one side of page. 25 scene plates for backgrounds. 6 collages by Harter, Satty, Singer, Evans. Introduction. 192pp. 8⅞ x 11¾. 23659-5 Pa. $4.50

MANUAL OF TRADITIONAL WOOD CARVING, edited by Paul N. Hasluck. Possibly the best book in English on the craft of wood carving. Practical instructions, along with 1,146 working drawings and photographic illustrations. Formerly titled *Cassell's Wood Carving*. 576pp. 6½ x 9¼. 23489-4 Pa. $7.95

THE PRINCIPLES AND PRACTICE OF HAND OR SIMPLE TURNING, John Jacob Holtzapffel. Full coverage of basic lathe techniques—history and development, special apparatus, softwood turning, hardwood turning, metal turning. Many projects—billiard ball, works formed within a sphere, egg cups, ash trays, vases, jardiniers, others—included. 1881 edition. 800 illustrations. 592pp. 6⅛ x 9¼. 23365-0 Clothbd. $15.00

THE JOY OF HANDWEAVING, Osma Tod. Only book you need for hand weaving. Fundamentals, threads, weaves, plus numerous projects for small board-loom, two-harness, tapestry, laid-in, four-harness weaving and more. Over 160 illustrations. 2nd revised edition. 352pp. 6½ x 9¼. 23458-4 Pa. $5.00

THE BOOK OF WOOD CARVING, Charles Marshall Sayers. Still finest book for beginning student in wood sculpture. Noted teacher, craftsman discusses fundamentals, technique; gives 34 designs, over 34 projects for panels, bookends, mirrors, etc. "Absolutely first-rate"—E. J. Tangerman. 33 photos. 118pp. 7¾ x 10⅝. 23654-4 Pa. $3.00

AMERICAN ANTIQUE FURNITURE, Edgar G. Miller, Jr. The basic coverage of all American furniture before 1840: chapters per item chronologically cover all types of furniture, with more than 2100 photos. Total of 1106pp. 7⅞ x 10¾. 21599-7, 21600-4 Pa., Two-vol. set $17.90

ILLUSTRATED GUIDE TO SHAKER FURNITURE, Robert Meader. Director, Shaker Museum, Old Chatham, presents up-to-date coverage of all furniture and appurtenances, with much on local styles not available elsewhere. 235 photos. 146pp. 9 x 12. 22819-3 Pa. $5.00

ORIENTAL RUGS, ANTIQUE AND MODERN, Walter A. Hawley. Persia, Turkey, Caucasus, Central Asia, China, other traditions. Best general survey of all aspects: styles and periods, manufacture, uses, symbols and their interpretation, and identification. 96 illustrations, 11 in color. 320pp. 6⅛ x 9¼. 22366-3 Pa. $6.00

CHINESE POTTERY AND PORCELAIN, R. L. Hobson. Detailed descriptions and analyses by former Keeper of the Department of Oriental Antiquities and Ethnography at the British Museum. Covers hundreds of pieces from primitive times to 1915. Still the standard text for most periods. 136 plates, 40 in full color. Total of 750pp. 5⅜ x 8½. 23253-0 Pa. $10.00

THE WARES OF THE MING DYNASTY, R. L. Hobson. Foremost scholar examines and illustrates many varieties of Ming (1368-1644). Famous blue and white, polychrome, lesser-known styles and shapes. 117 illustrations, 9 full color, of outstanding pieces. Total of 263pp. 6⅛ x 9¼. (Available in U.S. only) 23652-8 Pa. $6.00

ACKERMANN'S COSTUME PLATES, Rudolph Ackermann. Selection of 96 plates from the *Repository of Arts*, best published source of costume for English fashion during the early 19th century. 12 plates also in color. Captions, glossary and introduction by editor Stella Blum. Total of 120pp. 8⅜ x 11¼. 23690-0 Pa. $4.50

Prices subject to change without notice.

Available at your book dealer or write for free catalogue to Dept. GI, Dover Publications, Inc., 180 Varick St., N.Y., N.Y. 10014. Dover publishes more than 175 books each year on science, elementary and advanced mathematics, biology, music, art, literary history, social sciences and other areas.